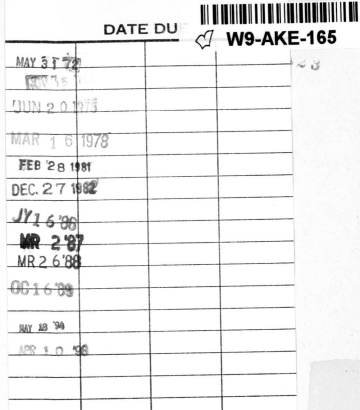

Can Small Business Survive?

CAN SMALL
BUSINESS SURVIVE?

SENATOR WILLIAM PROXMIRE

 Henry Regnery Company
Chicago   1964

Preface

If you're a small businessman, you're in big trouble and you know it. Whether you're a butcher, a baker, or a candlestick maker, you may soon be as extinct as the village blacksmith.

If you own "the little store around the corner" where people *used* to run in to shop, you know what a tough struggle it is to keep your head above water.

Newspaper headlines like these aren't news to you: "Failures on the Rise: Stiffer Competition Lifts Bankruptcy Rate to a 20-Year High"; "Business Failures Highest Since 1933"; "Small Business Declining in Area."

Your business may be the next to join these statistics. But it doesn't have to be. Your economic illness is curable. As in any long sickness, the road to recovery will be hard. It will demand your time, brain, imagination, skill, and judgment. You'll have to act.

This book is designed to help you act. In it you will find suggestions on how to improve your economic, managerial, and competitive position. You also will find information on where to get practical advice and assist-

5531

ance—from private agencies and from your local, state, and federal governments.

In the long pull, of course, your success or failure will not depend upon any outside help or lack of it, but squarely on you. You are the person who knows your own business best, and you probably are only too aware of your problems.

Can Small Business Survive? is, then, not so much a book to help you as it is a book to help you help yourself.

TABLE OF CONTENTS

WILL THE BIG BOYS CRUSH YOU?

CAN YOU SELL ABROAD?

WILL CONGRESS GO TO BAT FOR YOU?

Will The Small Businessman
Fade Away?

1

SMALL BUSINESS: BACK TO THE WALL

Have you thought about going into business for yourself? Do you want to own your own business? Be your own boss? Are you willing to take that chance with your future?

These are the big American questions.

At some time in their lives, as several nationwide surveys show, half of all American wage earners either attempt to go into business for themselves or intend to do so.

Many succeed in the attempt and realize the American dream of individual business enterprise and ownership. Indeed, some 95 per cent of the business community consists of small business proprietors. Most small businessmen and -women find, however, that being in business gives them neither the riches nor the independence they had expected. But they stick it out if they can, recognizing that other solid values and satisfactions make up for the long hours, the constant worries, the hard work, and often small financial return of small business proprietorship.

The Gams, for example, bought a small restaurant on the strength of Mr. Gam's twenty-nine years' experience as a fry cook. Confident in their ability to be managers and to run a restaurant profitably, they poured their savings of $2,000 and a bank loan of $15,000 into remodeling the premises.

The Gams opened as a seafood specialty house, hiring a chef and two waitresses. But after the first week, seeing that they were losing money, they had to make a hard decision. Either they had to close at once or sacrifice their dreams of being managers and do the work themselves. Choosing the latter course, Mr. and Mrs. Gam let the help go, appointing themselves chef and waitress.

The first year was a nightmare—two people trying to run a restaurant alone. But gradually the hard work began to pay off. The Gams experimented with the hours, advertised, rearranged the booths, and, in general, tried to be alert to every possible improvement.

Today their loan is paid off and the restaurant's future looks more promising. Some help has been hired, but Mr. and Mrs. Gam still are doing most of the work. They have had to revise their original ideas of what being in business would mean. In the Gams' case, the satisfactions of ownership and of using their ingenuity and creativity to build up a going business outweighed the difficulties posed by long hours and hard work. They stuck with their business, and are making a success of it.

But while many, like the Gams, do succeed, the sad fact is that hard work and ingenuity do not always pay off. Many more who go into business for themselves fail.

Let's look at the statistics. True enough, in terms of the total number of businesses now in operation, there are more individual firms today than at the turn of the century. At first glance this fact might seem to contradict all the evidence of business concentration and monopoly we hear so much about. The total number of business firms, however, would be bound to grow in view of the tremendous population increase this country has seen since 1900.

Moreover, the rapid rate of industrialization and the consequent move of rural people toward the city have also contributed to the growth of business in terms of over-all numbers. In 1820, for example, 72 per cent of Americans were employed in agriculture. By 1870 this had dropped to 53 per cent, and today only 9 per cent of the total labor force is in agriculture.

While the total number of business firms has continued its steady growth, we should by no means overlook the fact that the ownership and the durability of individual firms have become very unstable. Department of Commerce figures show that from 1955 through 1958 the number of individual business units increased by 302,000, from some 4.3 million to 4.6 million.

During this same period, however, 1.3 million concerns went out of business, and 1.6 million new establishments opened their doors! Moreover, 1.5 million firms changed ownership; of the 4.3 million in existence on January 1, 1955, only one-third were still doing business under the same management four years later. And no statistics exist to show how many in this remaining one-third are today teetering on the brink of failure, their owners earning only a bare subsistence.

Thus the steady increase in the total number of business firms conceals the startling and stubborn fact that most small businesses are struggling for their very survival.

What is a small business?

There have been any number of definitions, ranging from "all business that is not General Motors or United States Steel" to "the business where the owner does most of the work with his own hands, assisted by members of his family (most of the time unpaid) and/or by a few employees who function mainly as his assistants."

Depending on the industry, the federal Small Business Administration uses a 250 to 1,000-employee limitation for manufacturing concerns to define small business. In classifying wholesalers as small business, SBA uses annual sales of $5 million or less, and for construction concerns, $7.5 million. Annual sales of $1 million or less are used to classify most retailers, $2 million most grocers, and $1 million most service industries.

These definitions place 95 per cent of American business in the small business category. It is, however, in the 75 per cent of these, that are in an even smaller category, where the real problem lies.

Perhaps the definition contained in a letter to the Senate Small Business Committee from a filling-station operator in Georgia best sums up the kind of business-man whose back is literally against the wall—who most needs concerted assistance to strengthen and preserve his right to stay in business: "the little individually operated business, e.g., a grocery store, dry-goods store, filling station, shoe store, jewelry store, whose owner works himself, earns, or tries to, a small or fair living, and employs one or two people to assist him."

These small businesses are worth saving, not for rea-sons of nostalgia for the "mom and pop" store, but because they contribute to our society in ways that large corporations cannot. Small businessmen make many products and perform many services more efficiently and more economically than do large corporations, simply by the fact of *being* smaller, more flexible, and closer to the consumer.

This, of course, is not to say that large companies, with their marvelous techniques of mass production and distribution—techniques which bring so many wonder-ful products within the reach of the average man—do not also have their place in American life.

The fact is that the two types of business enterprise are complementary. *Both* the large corporation and the small business have distinct roles in the economic life of America. Somehow we seem to have lost sight of this simple fact. We have come to believe that business con-

7

centration and the giant corporation are the "modern" facts of business life, and that the take-over of all business enterprise by large corporations is inevitable. In this view, small business is a remnant of the horse-and-buggy age and should indeed be preserved—but as a museum piece. There is, however, no earthly reason why this should be so.

How can you aid small business?

What can you do to preserve and strengthen small business? Three things.

1. First of all, you must consciously and positively recognize what you, as a small businessman, contribute to American life.

For one thing, small firms provide two-fifths* of total employment. They account for 40 per cent of business activity. Some 50 million Americans—the owners, their employees and families—depend on small business for their livelihood.

Small business, therefore, is an important reservoir of job opportunities—particularly today, when we are facing the problems of automation in the large corporations. Here are businesses that do not lend themselves so readily to automation: personal service industries, small specialty manufacturing concerns, amusement concerns, recreational and tourist businesses, repair and spare parts shops, and specialty retailing firms.

---

* SBA statistical office estimates, October 31, 1963.

Further, we need small firms to preserve competition. Over half of all manufactured goods are now produced in industries in which the four largest manufacturers of each product control more than 50 per cent of the sales. This trend must be stemmed. Only a vigorous small business community can preserve our free competitive enterprise system in the face of these giants.

A healthy small business community can also counteract the dangers of inordinate political influence and control sometimes exercised by large corporations in an economy dominated by big fellows.

Besides providing a salutary balance for the large corporation, you and other small businessmen have a positive role in the communities you serve across the nation. Small enterprises still form the backbone of American democracy. In small cities, towns, and villages, besides meeting the material needs of the people, the small businessman represents the social, political, and moral leadership. It is the small businessman who provides the community spirit that builds and improves our towns, chambers of commerce, and Kiwanis and Lions clubs. The leadership, the time, the energy, and the money come from you and others like you.

Small business also nurtures commercial initiative and inventiveness. Many important innovations and advances in manufacturing, selling, and services have come from the small business sector. The development of plastics as major American products and the rapid growth of the electronics industry, with its amazing capacity to make life more comfortable and convenient for all of us, are two recent examples.

2. As a small businessman, you must be able to recognize and diagnose unhealthy symptoms in your business. To alleviate and cure the maladies these symptoms point to, you must be able to make use of the advice and assistance available to you—and this is an impressively large amount.

As a small businessman, you are likely to have many kinds of trouble: financial, managerial, and competitive. Although you may need a loan at two or three crucial times as your business expands, it is possible that you will lack opportunities for capital. Management troubles may threaten time and again. You may not have adequate protection under the laws designed to preserve competition. Although membership in a trade association may bring valuable suggestions, these suggestions may not be applicable to your business. You need more help and you must know where to go for it.

It is you, yourself, who live with the business and with its problems and difficulties day after day after day. And it is you who will do the actual "making or breaking."

This book is a good example of what I mean. In it I make many suggestions and tell you all about sources of advice and assistance. However, it still is up to you to evaluate these suggestions from your own point of view—and to act on them. No book, no agency, no consultant, no tax expert, no trade association, no United States senator can act for you.

3. Finally, in putting into effect this three-point program for small business, you must work diligently in the sectors where public policy is made. Small business, now discriminated against on so many fronts in favor of the large and powerful corporation, must once again have a chance to find its rightful place in the scheme of things.

The Senate Select Committee on Small Business has stated the problem of public policy toward small business in pointed fashion:

> Small business has failed to share on a relatively equal basis with big business in the present boom period. Equally disquieting is a lack of evidence that the future holds out to small businessmen any substantial hope that he, the quintessential expression of our free-enterprise system, may be able to maintain his position in an economy which offers mounting testimony that size and success, as well as size and survival, are correlative.

This book will deal with this three-point "survival program" for you and the millions of small businessmen like you.

2
LAUNCHING YOUR BUSINESS:
CRITICAL FIRST STEPS

You probably have a friend (maybe several) who started his own little shop or store a few years ago and then failed or quit. Why did he fail? Perhaps he was a shoe salesman. And a good one. But when he opened his own shoe store, nothing seemed to go right. Before long, his business was closed and he was back at his old job selling shoes.

If so, he is like many others. He got tired of working for somebody else and wanted to start out on his own. But he had only a hazy idea of the problems that would always be present in operating a business.

Unfortunately, the independence and security that come with operating a successful business don't just happen. To succeed, a business must be based on sound planning, the good judgment and character of the operator, long hours of hard work, and—more and more these days—on methodical record-keeping and use of those records.

If you are planning to start a business of your own or if you have just started in business, your success will depend on a series of critical first steps that you must take to give your business a solid foundation.

Aptitude

Before starting out, however, you must make a decision which may be the most crucial of all; you must decide whether you have what it takes to succeed.

It is a plain fact that some people are not suited, either by temperament or by desire to succeed, to go into business for themselves. Although self-appraisal is sometimes difficult, if you are planning to start a new business you should make an honest effort to look at yourself objectively. The ability to withstand the frustrations and disappointments that come with starting a new business, the ability to work long hours, the ability to get along with employees and the public, and the honest desire to make a success of the new business are traits that, along with good business judgment, must be present before a new business can grow and prosper.

Having made the decision to launch yourself into business, your first step is to determine how much capital you will need. This is not easy. Calculate realistically how much over-all income you expect from your business the first year, the first two years, and the first three years, with top and bottom limits. Make a complete estimate of your expenses during those periods and add a margin for unexpected developments.

Then, set down how much actual cash you can afford to invest in your business. Make a list of any assets that you can sell, or on which you can borrow. Make a list of other sources which will lend you money on reasonable terms. You should also plan to have a cash reserve to take care of an unexpected drop in revenues or an increase in expenses. And, right off the bat, talk over your plans with your banker and get his suggestions.

The absence of adequate capital has dealt the death blow to thousands of new businesses. It is a major stumbling-block to success. Many men go into business on a shoestring. They do not have enough money of their own in the business at the beginning to take care of its very minimum needs. They borrow. The only capital generally available has short terms and high interest. Long-term loans and ownership capital are very difficult for a new small business to obtain.

The repayment of these short-term loans can cause a serious drop in your cash at a time when you can least afford it, when you need your cash for the day-to-day operating expenses of your business. The burden of repaying immediate indebtedness not only is bad for the financial structure of your concern, but it will stop you from operating an aggressive, expanding business, ready to take advantage of ripe opportunities. You will have enough to worry about in keeping your business going without being hounded by creditors.

Records

Keep careful records. Hire your local accountant to set up a complete record system. You'll find this an excellent investment. You will need accurate records for tax purposes. They are also necessary to support any loan application you may want to make.

15

But, most important, records will keep you accurately informed on the state of your business. You cannot make wise management decisions unless you have a clear knowledge of your financial condition. For instance, this knowledge will help you decide whether you should buy new machinery or sell part of what you have, whether to hire or reduce the number of employees. A good, up-to-date financial record of your company can be one of your best management friends.

Lack of good financial records caused by disinterest in record-keeping can result in bankruptcy.

After graduation from high school and service in the army, John Armitage opened a retail store in a small town in Wisconsin. The store carried the usual variety of merchandise found in small town retail stores: clothing, household goods, farm equipment, and feed for livestock.

John ran the store with the help of a woman clerk. He dealt with wholesalers and attended to all financial transactions. He compiled returns for social security and for local, state, and federal taxes.

Busy and confident of his success as a businessman, John did well at the tasks he tackled. But he made a nearly fatal mistake. After a couple of years he noted a sharp increase in his sales of farm equipment and this required a bigger outlay for inventory. To his surprise, he discovered that he would have trouble getting the necessary financing for the increase in stock. The bank wanted to see his business records before making a loan. He had none.

At the suggestion of his bank, John hired a competent accountant to make a complete survey of his business and to set up a bookkeeping system. The accountant discovered that while farm machinery sales were improving, Armitage was, in fact, losing money because of improper pricing. This information caused John to revise his business operations completely. He limited his own activities to sales and hired a full-time bookkeeper.

John is certain that the establishment of a sound accounting system saved him from bankruptcy. Because so few small businesses have financial records, and fewer still use them aggressively, such records can give you a sure competitive advantage.

Location

Whether you are going into the retail business or plan to operate a small manufacturing plant, the location of your business is of prime importance. In choosing the location for a small manufacturing plant, you should consider adequate access to raw materials, to customers, to labor supply, and to highway and rail facilities. High transportation costs can break you, and low costs can give you a solid competitive advantage.

Locating a retail store or filling station demands a careful check of the proposed neighborhood. Make a traffic count on the street in question and study the movement of pedestrians and cars in the area. Make sure that your location is close to your customers, women and men who will pay to buy what you sell.

17

Be sure to find out whether urban renewal plans are being made for the area. Decide whether the neighborhood is growing or declining by checking the census to see how many people live in the area, and how many lived there ten and twenty years ago.

By all means choose the location with the success of your business in mind, and not from any personal feelings you may have about the area. Do not select it merely because you are familiar with that part of the city, because it is convenient to your home, or because there is an existing business for sale there. That business may be for sale because the location is poor.

Competition

Consider competition before you locate in an area. Make sure that the business you plan is needed and has a reasonable chance for success. How? Interview the suppliers and wholesalers with whom you will do business in order to get their opinions. Ask what kind of service you will get from them if you open in their area. Some new businesses have found that suppliers to established firms are hesitant to supply a new customer for fear of losing their good, established ones.

Verifying a need for your business in the neighborhood means a thorough check, not just a casual stroll up the street. Failure to make an intelligent study of expected competition can result in a more serious failure.

Mary Baker, a middle-aged widow, received a modest

amount of money from her husband's insurance policy. Her children were married and lived in a nearby city.

Mrs. Baker was determined to keep her independence and not to be a burden on her children. She had a "green thumb," and during her early married life had won prizes with her roses in the local garden club's contests. With this love and knowledge of flowers, she was immediately interested in an opportunity to rent a store which could easily be converted into a flower shop. She also decided to carry a line of greeting cards and other novelties.

Mrs. Baker thought she had chosen an ideal location. She was near a large shopping center (not containing a flower shop), and on the edge of a new, growing community of medium-priced homes.

After leasing the store and purchasing supplies, Mrs. Baker opened a shop. It didn't take long for her to discover that she had not been careful enough in her selection of the site. She found that the supermarket in the shopping center regularly carried a small line of cut flowers, and that at Easter it carried almost as complete a stock as she did. And the drugstore carried a line of cards that was much more complete than hers.

This competition was too much for Baker's Flower Shop. Mrs. Baker was forced to close. The story has a happy ending, however, since the supermarket hired her to run its flower section. She is saving her money and plans to try again—this time after a more careful check of her competition.

Merchandising and raw materials

In your new business you will find that one of the most difficult management problems is merchandising. The type and the variety of goods with which you stock your store must satisfy customers. Your record system will indicate just how far you can afford to go in building your inventory. Success depends on a careful balance between stock on hand and sales volume. Keep the fast-moving products in ample supply. Promptly weed out the slow items. You can't afford to tie up your limited money in a large, sluggish inventory.

An adequate—but no more than adequate—supply of raw materials is vital to a manufacturing concern in order to avoid costly delays in filling orders. Promptness in delivery of orders is one of the best ways to establish customers' confidence in your new firm. This confidence not only will lead to additional business, but it will enhance your reputation for reliability as well. Calculate your inventory so that you tie up as little capital as possible. Cost records will make it possible for you to do this.

Prices and overhead costs

You will also find that you have to give careful study to the prices charged for your products and merchandise. Prices must be sufficient to cover all your costs, which in turn must be low enough to permit those prices to meet competition. You know what your costs really are if you have kept complete records. If your costs are high you are in a position to act, for you know what costs have been rising. You can fight to get them under control.

Advertising

Advertising can also play an important role in the success or failure of your new concern. There are various media: newspapers, radio, television, the yellow pages of the telephone book, and direct mail advertising.

Then your records, along with inquiry of your customers, will tell you what advertising is paying off. You can decide how much you can or wish to spend on it. You'll have a solid factual basis for expanding the advertising that pays off and promptly killing that which doesn't.

Charge accounts

Should you encourage your customers to open charge accounts, or should you operate solely on cash? Some new, small retail stores and filling stations have found that the use of credit is necessary to keep them in business. The customers expect it and will trade only with those concerns which grant it. If you extend credit, keep careful records of its cost to you. Many firms have succeeded famously by going on a strictly cash basis and passing on much of their savings to customers.

21

If you decide on credit, you will have to use discretion in granting it and use hardhearted, businesslike methods in collecting debts due. If you let credit accounts go unpaid for any length of time, you will find that they become unmanageable. Stay alert, then, to all delinquent accounts, and start your collection process right away. You must realize that even with adequate capital you cannot long remain solvent if your debtors fail to pay their bills.

To sum up

Each of the factors which we have discussed in this chapter represents a matter of good business judgment on your part. Each of these or a combination of them can cause the failure or the lack of success of your business. Errors of judgment in these areas can be corrected either by outside help or as the result of experience.

So again, to a great extent the success or failure of your business depends on you. You may find that the personal satisfaction of owning and operating your own business is worth all the effort it takes. You may not. One thing you can be sure of. The effort demanded is very great indeed. And it must be constant.

Where Do You Get The Money?

3

THE NUMBER ONE PROBLEM:
ENOUGH MONEY

The inability of small business to obtain needed capital has been the concern of businessmen and the government for many years. The greatest needs of small businessmen are for ownership capital and long-term loans.

The plight of Mrs. Gates is typical. For as long as she could remember, she had wanted her own business. In the light of her twenty-one years of experience as a waitress, she decided to open a dinette. A $3,500 bank loan together with $400 of her savings covered the launching: remodeling, furnishing, and initial stocking. And she still had $750 left over for operating capital. "If the dinette pays me $200 a month in the clear, I'll be satisfied," Mrs. Gates declared on opening day.

For the first couple of months Gates' Dinette experienced the rush all new restaurants attract. The new owner was pleased to see that she did net $200 above expenses the first month—but not so pleased to find she had to pay out $100 on her short-term bank loan.

By the end of the second month, the initial rush was over and Mrs. Gates' income plummeted. But the bank loan still had to be paid, and during the third and fourth months she netted only enough to cover the loan payments and her overhead, with nothing left over for herself. Having invested an additional $1,000 during the months she was open, she was forced to close after six months—with a loss of over $4,000.

Gates' Dinette illustrates very well the key difficulty you'll face in getting started. Short-term credit will not be hard to get, but the burden of repaying loans before the business has returned a sufficient flow of profit in most cases turns out to be overwhelming.

Years ago, even small business could depend on earnings to provide most of its capital needs. The Ford Motor Company is a prime example of the successful growth of a small business, from a one-man toolshed to a giant corporation. And Henry Ford achieved a great part of this growth through turning back almost every dollar he earned into his business.

Since World War II, however, expansion through retained earnings has become more difficult, especially for small business. Higher taxes immediately take away a big chunk of the profits, while ever-soaring equipment costs demand a higher level of capital expenditure for efficient production. Without that efficiency, no businessman can compete for long—either against his local counterparts or against foreign producers. At the very time when business capital requirements are greatest, therefore, retained profits are minimal.

The possibilities for raising money

If your firm competes with big business, you have to recognize immediately that the big fellow has the advantage in getting capital. Getting short-term credit probably won't be too much of a problem for you, but obtaining long-term loans and persuading others to invest with you as co-owners will be. If big business is not losing money, it gets capital automatically through its depreciation reserves. Typically, it also retains and reinvests a big share of its earnings. Usually it has no trouble borrowing long-term money or selling stock to the public.

What, then, are the possibilities open to you?

You may be able to finance your business with your own savings or with loans from your family and close friends. Government statistics show that most new businesses are dependent primarily upon the savings of the owner and his family. But these dollars are limited.

Your bank can supply short-term loans. But banks generally won't lend you money for more than five years, for reasons of public policy and the prudent rules of commercial banking. Suppliers and other private lenders may also be good sources of short-term credit.

If your bank turns you down and you have a sound basis for borrowing, you can borrow from the federal Small Business Administration.

The SBA was specifically designed to provide services to small business, the most important of these being to extend to small business regular loans with maturities up to ten years. The specifics of securing such loans are discussed in Chapter 5. Other federal agencies either make or guarantee loans to small businessmen. A compilation of these sources has recently been published in a booklet entitled *Federal Handbook for Small Business,* available free from the Small Business Administration, Washington 25, D.C.

What about institutional lenders? A series of studies has shown that institutional lenders such as insurance companies and pension funds, with enormous amounts of money to lend or invest, have committed only an insignificant amount to small and independent business over the past fifteen years. Perhaps they should not be criticized for this. They hold their money in strict trust and are seldom able to supervise closely a large number of small businesses, while they can disburse the same amount of money to one big corporation with minimum risk and trouble.

I'll have more to say about all these possibilities in this and in the two chapters following.

Other possibilities

Despite the very great disadvantage that small business suffers in the capital market, there are methods for you to obtain the ready capital you need to start out or to meet unexpected emergencies. A sudden upsurge in orders, for example, may require the purchase of additional machinery or supplies; you may have to put employees on overtime or hire additional employees to fill them. Or you may find you have reached a plateau, where you must either expand or reconcile yourself to a profit return which may not at all be proportionate to the potential of your business.

Dick Grooms had just this experience. A young pharmacist with a year's experience in filling prescriptions for another drugstore, Dick opened his own store in 1958. His father helped him out by buying the building in which he wanted to locate and renting it to him for $100 a month. Dick was able to borrow enough from his bank on a short-term basis to remodel and stock his store.

Business during the first two months was as good as Dick could have expected. But the next four months saw no increase, and Dick sensed that he had reached a point where he was marking time, and not progressing toward a real "take-off."

Dick was not afraid of advice, and asked everyone whose opinion he valued—his former employer, his suppliers, certain of his customers—how he might improve his business. The concensus seemed to point to the installation of a soda fountain. Hoping to build his business around his prescriptions, Dick had not originally intended to have a fountain. But he was flexible enough to change his mind when his customers seemed to expect it.

Not wanting to deplete the liquid reserves he needed for his day-to-day operations, Dick faced the problem of raising $2,000 to install the fountain. He had already gone the limit with his bank and his father, so he turned to his supplier. Impressed with Dick's ability and the store's potential, the supplier agreed to rearrange Dick's payment schedule on drugs he had already purchased and, in addition, lent him $750 to make the down payment on fountain equipment.

With the added revenue the fountain immediately brought in, Dick has been able—though it took a rough year to see daylight—to honor his original obligations and pay off the balance on the soda fountain equipment and the supplier's loan. Now the added revenue is money in his pocket, and Dick is off the plateau.

With good management practices and skillful operating procedures, money can be obtained in a short time. A good cost-accounting system and a complete record of sales will help persuade your banker or others to lend to you.

If you want funds without a bank loan, you can: (1) halt temporarily the purchase of raw materials not immediately needed; (2) determine if any production speed-up is possible without overtime, so that the product can be sold ahead of schedule; (3) attempt to readjust, after consultation with the Internal Revenue Service, your tax burden by changes in depreciation schedules and inventory accounting; (4) eliminate, as far as possible, any backlog products by a speed-up in delivery; (5) attempt to arrange with suppliers, as Dick Grooms did, a stretching out of payment schedules.

Another method for raising needed cash capital is

the factor, an individual or company which will buy accounts receivable from your business, charging a specified commission. The factor then deals directly with the creditor in collecting the account.

You might also consider taking on a partner, who may or may not be active in the business, to bring in additional capital. Or if your business is a corporation you might consider selling stock to secure permanent equity capital.

Many businessmen are reluctant to sell stock in their companies, not only because it is an expensive way to obtain capital, but also for fear that their control of the business will be jeopardized. Of course, it is not necessary to offer more stock to the public than you retain; you do not have to lose control of your company.

However, you should be well aware of the costs that will be involved in obtaining capital in this manner. There will be costs involved in preparing information for the registration statement and prospectus required by the Securities and Exchange Commission, in fees for the underwriters, lawyers, accountants, and for other professional services, as well as in administrative expenses.

Generally, the smaller you are and the less capital you wish to raise the more expensive your rate of stock will be, since the cost of issuing stock, whether a great or small number of shares, remains relatively constant. Unless you are prepared to raise several million dollars, issuing stock is likely to be too costly a method.

An enterprising young man in the Southwest found—to his dismay—how expensive it is to "go public" and issue stock in his company. Immediately after World War II, John Jennings entered a new industry—the sale of propane gas and equipment. He started his business with a $3,000 investment. Sales for the first year's operation were $46,000, and by 1956 his sales had grown to $2 million per year.

For the first few years his bankers were not convinced that the propane gas business would succeed. They refused to supply John with any type of financing, not even short-term. After three or four years, however, his bankers were willing to provide limited short-term financing for the sale of his gas tanks and appliances.

By 1955, John was so successful that he needed long-term financing to expand his business. His only access to this type of financing was through the sale of stock. Unable to interest any brokers in his state, John was forced to go to New York to find a brokerage house to handle his securities.

He had to devote considerable expense and time to the sale of his stock, over and above the actual brokerage fees, attorneys' fees, and so on. The complete issue was for $700,000, but the net amount John obtained was $575,000. Thus the issue cost him $125,000—a terrifically high cost.

Sufficient capital on the right terms remains one of the most severe restrictions on small business formation and growth. But as I have indicated, there are methods of obtaining capital which, with ingenuity, you may be able to use to your advantage.

Studies of small business credit problems—the SBIC

For more than thirty years, experts have been studying the money-raising problems of small businessmen like you. The first important study was made in England in 1931 by a committee headed by Harold Macmillan, later Prime Minister of Great Britain. This committee discovered that small business in England could not raise the capital it required even when the security it offered was sound. This lack of borrowing opportunities was called the Macmillan Gap.

Similar studies were later made in this country. In 1935 the United States Department of Commerce surveyed 6,158 manufacturers in all parts of the country. These manufacturers employed between twenty-one and 250 employees. The survey found that 47.2 per cent of them could not get long-term funds from any source whatever, even though examination of their financial statements indicated that two-thirds of them could be considered sound credit risks.

Shortly after World War II, the Committee for Economic Development made a study of small business problems. After its study it concluded:

> One of the fundamental needs of small and medium-size business is more adequate financing. More long-term credit

is needed relative to short-term. . . . More ownership funds are needed relative to borrowed funds. . . . Present banking facilities should be supplemented to open up, for the small enterprise, channels for capital loans and equity capital. The Committee for Economic Development suggests the formation of new capital banks for this purpose.

Congress first became interested in the problems of long-term small business financing in 1949. The Joint Committee on the Economic Report made a study of the volume and stability of private investments and the role of the federal government in promoting the investment of capital. The committee concluded that study should be given to what steps can and should be taken "to preserve an open door for investment in little and local business in terms of ownership as well as in terms of debt."

In 1952 the Federal Reserve Board made a study of small business problems for the Senate Select Committee on Small Business, and in 1955 the Department of Commerce made a further study of small business financing. In June, 1957, the Senate Banking and Currency Committee, and in November, 1957, the House Select Committee on Small Business, held hearings and received further evidence of the seriousness of the credit needs of small business.

In April, 1958, the Federal Reserve Board completed a year-long study of small business credit. After a complete review of the problem, Chairman William McChesney Martin told the Senate Banking and Currency Committee that "there is room for a government program to foster the flow of private investment funds to small business."

Based on this solid evidence of need, several congressmen, including myself, introduced the Small Business Investment Act of 1958, which was passed in August of that year. This act provides for the licensing by the Small Business Administration of private companies (called Small Business Investment Companies) designed to furnish equity and long-term loans to small business. I'll go into much more detail about the SBICs in Chapter 6.

4

CAN THE BANKERS DO A
BIGGER JOB?

If you've ever gone to your local banker with a
major financial problem, the chances are that you've
found him surprisingly knowledgeable about your business and very sympathetic to your plight, but exceed-
ingly reluctant to relieve your situation in the most
obvious way—by handing over the long-term cash you
need at a reasonable rate of interest.

Your situation may be very like that of Joe Wilson,
an energetic young fellow who owns a job-printing
shop in Wisconsin. Joe wanted to expand his services
by investing in a high-speed offset press. He needed
modern equipment, not only to improve his work and
get new customers, but also to compete with a new,
modern printing plant which had opened at the county
seat, twelve miles away. His financial history was excellent and his credit rating tops.

"It was obvious to me that I had to have this press
to stay in business," Joe recalls. "It also was clear that
I'd be able to meet the payments and interest regularly

—but that the payments would have to be spread out some because while my business is regular, the volume in a one-man operation obviously isn't tremendous.

"Our local banker knew all this—and he knew me. I went to high school with him, and we go to the same church and belong to the same lodge. In fact, I'd discussed the new press with him at lodge meeting only the week before."

So Joe dropped by his bank one day with the order form for the new press, filled in and ready to mail.

"Bernard," Joe said to his friend, "I need $14,000 for that new press I told you about and some other equipment I'm ordering from Chicago. I can pay you back $100 a month, plus interest. Or even $125 a month, if you think that would work out better."

Joe felt that he could afford the higher payment because he had asked around and knew that his work would pick up when he had the new equipment on his floor. In fact he even had dreams of bidding on the printing of the county weekly newspaper.

"Was I naïve!" says Joe now. "But I'd never had any occasion to deal with a bank before except to balance my checking account and look after my savings once in a while. Imagine my surprise when Bernard began to get that look I've since come to associate with the banker's bedside manner. He tried to let me down easy— imagine, me, who'd never owed anyone in that town a nickel!"

"I'm sorry," Bernard told Joe. "It can't be done. That comes out to a ten-year loan."

"Of course it does," Joe shot back. "I can multiply —and that's what I'm asking for: a ten-year loan."

"I could give you twenty-four or even thirty-six months—and try to renew," the banker offered.

"Except you know I could never pay it back in such a short time."

"We're just a small bank," Bernard explained. "We don't have huge amounts of money on hand. We have to keep our money active and get a quick return on it. We just can't afford to have so much tied up in long-term loans." Nor did Joe fare any better when he tried the larger bank at the county seat.

As the previous chapters indicate, Joe Wilson's disappointing experience is not unusual. Most small businesses have a tough time getting long-term financing from their local bankers. Although Federal Reserve Board surveys show that banks and the large wholesale trade suppliers extend most of the loans and credit small business receives, this financial assistance is given almost entirely on a short-term basis.

Why aren't the banks doing a bigger job for small business? What are their reasons for granting comparatively few long-term, small business loans—when some 95 per cent of all business in the United States has been classified as small?

Why are even intermediate-term loans being reduced from ten years to five or six years?

When small businessmen do succeed in getting a loan, why is the interest almost invariably higher for them than for their large competitors? And why must they put up collateral when their big business counterparts can get unsecured loans?

Why does the Small Business Administration often—contrary to its function as a supplemental source—loan to businesses that commercial banks ought to be serving? Surely banks could play a greater part in small business financing than just automatically granting the one or two turn-downs necessary for SBA application. Mr. David Rockefeller of the Chase Manhattan Bank, one of the largest banks in the world, strongly feels that a large portion of SBA loans could be handled by the banking industry.

Why aren't banks filling the equity gap? Can't they do a bigger job?

First let's look at the bankers' side of all these questions. Like Joe Wilson's friend Bernard, most small bankers do have a problem in extending long-term credit to small business. The commercial banks, indeed, are virtually the only organized financial institutions extending credit to small business at all.

Even these banks, however, must keep their loans in fairly liquid form in order to meet the needs of depositors, who may call for their funds at any time. This means that most banks deal almost exclusively in short-term and, on occasion, medium-term loans.

Moreover, bankers maintain that it is only recently that small business has been seeking long-term credit from commercial banks in significant amounts. They say, therefore, that techniques for dealing with such credit are not well developed. For example, the smaller banks have neither the time nor the skilled officers for the years of supervision and counsel that small business borrowers would require if they received long-term loans.

Finally, bankers say that they have to charge higher interest rates to small business because the mechanics of making loans to the little fellow simply cost more, in relation to the dollars involved, than for the large organization.

"We have the same costs—investigation, keeping books on the loan, and collection—with the small fellow as with the big borrower," they maintain. "This overhead, in the case of little business, has to be spread over a much smaller base.

"Indeed, to investigate a large business with well-kept records may actually cost less than to look into the financial position of a small business with indifferent or poor records. Naturally, the interest charge has to be higher for the small business loan."

All this banker's logic may sound reasonable enough, but it is small comfort to a man like Joe Wilson, who has nowhere to turn but to his banker, and who finds that—even though both he and his banker *know* he's a good risk—there is no money available for him.

In spite of the difficulties bankers face in granting credit to small business, they could do a bigger job. Indeed, the real hope for long-term small business money would seem to lie with local banks, for they are established institutions with many built-in assets as capital sources for small business.

After all, they are already going concerns—there would be no need to set up elaborate parallel structures to finance small business needs if bankers would expand their services to do the job. Also, they know their prospective small business customers better than any non-local financial agency can ever hope to. Moreover, they know local business conditions—this is crucial to sound judgment on individual business loans.

Local bankers also have a vested interest in the economic growth and prosperity of their own communities, in which small business plays an extremely important part. Local bankers are in the best position to assure a healthy and progressive small business sector.

What, specifically, can bankers do to help small business?

Liberalization of loan policies

A logical first step would seem to be for bankers to liberalize their loan policies—in line, of course, with rules of prudence and sound banking practice.

A recent survey of Wisconsin banks shows that policies toward small businesses differ widely. It shows that over half of Wisconsin banks make some loans to small business for equipment needs, working capital, and plant improvement. However, one-twentieth of these banks do not make loans at all to finance small business growth! And less than one-fourth are willing to make maturities of five years and over. This survey would seem to indicate that the banking community could indeed reappraise its approach to small business and come up with policies a little less weighted toward fiscal conservatism. If some banks within a state can profitably pursue a more liberal policy toward small business, there is no sound reason why more of them could not be doing so.

It is clear, of course, that since most funds in small banks come from demand deposits, a liberalization of loan policies toward small business can only be a partial solution. Obviously a bank cannot tie up all its funds in long-term loans to local small businesses; this would be unsound. Nevertheless, there are indications that even very small banks might well reappraise their long-term loan policies.

For example, I have not noticed banks shying away from the home mortgage field. In fact, there is a healthy competition among banks for these loans, even though they tie up money anywhere from fifteen to twenty-five years!

In this connection, what about the correspondent system? There must be something drastically wrong with it if smaller banks cannot turn to their correspondent banks, with their ready reserves, and receive money for small business loans as they do for mortgages.

Bankers also ask, "Why should we loan money to small business when we know we can make more money from other sources?" "Let's face it," they say, "small business loans just are not profitable."

I am reminded that bankers also said the same thing

43

about FHA Title One financing. At first they didn't think that was profitable, either. Now many offer their home improvement loans, almost identical to FHA—only without the government insurance.

There are also good opportunities for bankers to help out on long-term, small business financing by participating in Small Business Administration loans, either by providing the 10 per cent capital minimum, or by providing up to 25 per cent and higher using the new, streamlined short form application, which cuts the paper work involved. Also, individual banks could be allowed to invest more in SBICs. The amount now is fixed at 2 per cent, and it could be substantially higher.

Banks might also take a hard look at their standards for judging creditworthiness, and sometimes take bigger chances when the prospects for success are good.

For example, four young men had the opportunity to purchase a small data processing company near Washington, D.C., along with the one government contract it possessed. By mortgaging their homes, cashing in on their insurance, and pooling every possible resource, they managed to scrape together the $35,000 to buy it.

But now that they owned it, how were they going to run it? Even with the active government contract, they found they did not have enough capital to keep the business running. What could they do?

After receiving a cold shoulder from the SBA, they turned to Riggs National Bank, in the District. Fortunately James Bridges, vice-president in charge of loans, had the foresight to realize the great growth potential of this small company. Even though, undeniably, its start was somewhat shaky, he decided to go all the way with them and grant a $10,000 loan.

In ten short years this little company has grown from a firm with thirty-two employees and assets of $37,210 to an industry employing 883 people in eleven different countries, with total assets of nearly $11 million.

This is, no doubt, a spectacular example. But it illustrates the fact that there are thousands of small businesses throughout the nation with tremendous potential which are being held back because the financial agencies which most logically could help them are refusing to.

Government and government-related agencies can help in solving this equity gap. But the prosperity and growth of the nation will still be seriously inhibited until private financial institutions—principally the commercial banks—begin to do the job which is so obviously cut out for them.

5

CAN YOU GET A GOVERNMENT LOAN?

Dear Senator Proxmire:

Getting a loan from the Small Business Administration is like getting a case before the Supreme Court. Months of time and many dollars were spent before we could get even a loan application.

Sincerely,
BOB JAMES

Sound frustrated, and perhaps a little embittered? Does Bob James' problem sound like one you may have had? Bob James and others like him have this experience all too often.

Bob is a hard-working young man, short on money and long on ideas. He wants to make a profit and contribute something to the community at the same time. To do this, Bob and his partner decided to set up Crestview Acres, a housing development for elderly people. They bought fifty acres of property, along with old, out-dated housing that needed complete rebuilding.

The proposed retirement village was to be located in a small community on the edge of Wisconsin's resort country. The housing Bob and his partner envisioned would be suitable, however, for year-round living or for summer residence, in the case of elderly people who winter in the South. On his initial visit to my office, Bob outlined his difficulties with the Small Business Administration:

"Five months ago, my partner Joe Jacobs and I visited the SBA branch office nearest home," he told me. "We did so at the suggestion of the president of our local national bank, Mr. Richard Oleson. Mr. Oleson is, as you know, an extremely conservative man who views each loan application as if the money were actually his own.

"We talked with one of the employees of the SBA, who questioned our eligibility before knowing the facts. We told this representative of SBA that this was merely a call to obtain information. Joe and I wanted to know what the criteria were in order to secure some assistance. We said we were paying our call at the suggestion of a local banker, who was willing to assume twenty-five per cent of our loan."

Bob paused. "What happened then?" I asked encouragingly.

"Our SBA official said, 'Listen, Mr. James, before I give you a loan application I want your profit and loss statements for the past three years and a statement of prospects for the next six years. This information must be prepared by your accountants.'

"So Joe and I went home to get this stuff prepared, and two days later we returned with all the requested information to SBA. We were assured we would be hearing from them in the next two or three days. But two weeks passed and our need for assistance grew pressing. So we called the SBA and were told that the information had been turned over to another employee, and that this employee, B, was out of town for a long Fourth of July holiday."

"Did you finally get to see your man?" I asked.

"Joe and I made a forty mile trip to visit with employee B. He informed us that he had not seen the material. His secretary tried to locate it but was not successful. Luckily for Joe and me, we had an extra set of the requested information."

"So you presented it then and there?"

"Yes. But imagine our surprise when we were told that *additional* information was needed. Employee B asked us for a written history of the operations to date, a written explanation of the uses the money would be put to, complete financial statements, and personal histories of all stockholders, plus an independent appraisal of the collateral being offered."

Bob and Joe provided this additional material—at a total cost of some $500 for the accountant's fee, phone calls, and trips to the SBA branch office. I wish I could tell you that this remarkably persevering young man finally was rewarded with an SBA loan, but he wasn't. Rarely have I seen a case more deserving, in terms of initiative of the applicant, the soundness of the proposed business, and the utility of that business to the community.

After months of effort on his part, however, and my office's months-long attempt to go to bat for him, Bob finally got his money—but not from the SBA. He's built Crestview into a thriving new industry which now houses seventy persons, the majority over fifty years of age, and there will be 150 full-time residents by the time you read this.

Bob and Joe also are installing recreational facilities, which will include a four-acre lake and a nine-hole golf course. In an area classified by the Labor Department as "depressed," Bob and Joe are bringing in people who have income to spend in the neighboring towns and villages. Moreover, the new residents are at an age where they place no extra burdens on the labor market or the schools.

At the same time that Bob's SBA loan was pending, the SBA granted $150,000 to the prospective proprietors of a new motel in Bob's community! It is difficult to understand the SBA's evaluation of prospective small business borrowers, which leaves Bob out in the cold while treating the proprietors of a certainly less than essential business so handsomely.

What does the foregoing story of one little fellow's unfortunate experience with the SBA program mean? I wish I could say "Go ahead and try—Bob's case was exceptional." But there are just too many cases like his —of patiently deserving small businessmen who are losing out to motels, bowling alleys, and other non-essential businesses—for me to gloss over them, leaving you with the impression that your need for capital is going to be met swiftly by the SBA. Very likely it won't be. There is, of course, another side to the SBA story, to be discussed later on in this chapter.

Let's stop here for the moment and look at the SBA itself. What did Congress have in mind in setting it up? Congress has long recognized small business's financing problems, but it wasn't until 1953 that it took definite action. In that year it created the Small Business Administration—a successor, to some degree, to the old Reconstruction Finance Corporation. In 1958 the Small Business Act made the SBA a permanent executive agency.

Under the original concept, SBA's primary function was to give financial counseling to the small businessman and to lend money to small business enterprises which could not obtain funds on reasonable terms from private sources. At first the ceiling on SBA loans was $100,000; later this was upped to $250,000 and, still later, to $350,000—over my strong protests, I might add. The SBA was also to be the agency to which you and other small businessmen could look for information and assistance on management problems, and for help in getting a fair share of government contracts. These particular functions of SBA are detailed in Chapter 10.

The fight which SBA has waged to push up its loan ceiling is just one indication that it is not wholeheartedly oriented to the problems of the truly *small* businessman, and that it spends entirely too much effort and money on larger enterprises. There has been a definite tendency for SBA to become a medium-size or even a big business administration.

Moreover, the SBA lends to businesses which I consider to be definitely on the fringe, insofar as their real value to the community is concerned. Of course there is nothing wrong with bowling alleys, poolrooms, or motels. But I can not see how an argument can be made for giving federal assistance to such recreational industries when constructive projects, which serve the community on a much more long-range basis, are left to go a-begging.

Having painted such a gloomy picture, I should certainly not want to discourage you from trying for an SBA loan if you think you qualify—and, incidentally, letting your senator or congressman know if you feel you are not getting fair treatment.

Who is eligible for SBA funds? Just about any small business needing money for construction, conversion, or expansion, for the purchase of equipment, facilities, or supplies, or just for working capital. Loan applicants include small manufacturers, retailers, wholesalers, and service establishments.

What must you do to obtain a loan from the SBA? Before you can apply, you must first attempt to get financing privately. Your smartest initial move then, in nearly every case, is to go to your banker and lay your problems before him. He can tell you whether or not he can make a loan to you, and on what terms. If your bank is not able to go the full amount, your banker may still be willing to participate in the SBA loan at or beyond the minimum of 10 per cent.

I should warn you beforehand that in some communities bankers are extremely wary of SBA—or downright hostile. There is, however, little reason for banks to be suspicious of SBA or to regard it as competitive. For the SBA is designed to move into those areas where banks simply cannot, because of legal restrictions, grant long-term loans. The two agencies should, therefore, function in a complementary fashion, without any hint of competition. In many communities the banks and the SBA do work in fruitful partnership—as government and private initiative always should.

At the same time you get in touch with your banker, you should write the Small Business Administration in Washington for the name of your local SBA office, and for a copy of the SBA booklet *SBA Business Loans,* which will give you much useful information in preparing your loan presentation.

After studying the literature and deciding that you qualify for a loan, you should prepare an operating statement for the past three to five years, together with a clear presentation of your financial needs, the exact use to which the funds will be put, and the manner in which you intend to pay off the loan. It is on the basis of these documents that the SBA will decide whether or not to give you a loan application.

Since the SBA is lending the public's money, it is only right that they exercise care and caution in determining whether you have sufficient collateral to cover the loan, or a long-term earning record indicating that you can repay. My own objections to SBA procedure certainly do not have to do with its need to exercise ordinary care in extending financial assistance.

But let me emphasize *"ordinary."* For the SBA exists, after all, to fill the credit gap, and this purpose is thwarted when local SBA officials assume an attitude of extreme fiscal conservatism. I have seen case after case where local bankers—very much like Bob James' Mr. Oleson, who, as Bob observed, regards his bank's money as though it came out of his own pocket—had enough faith in local enterprise to be willing to participate up to 25 per cent in a loan, only to have SBA turn down the applicant for reasons of fiscal caution.

Maximum interest on SBA loans is fixed at 5.5 per cent. If your bank participates, it may charge a slightly higher rate on its portion of the loan; but the rate should be reasonable.

If you've studied the loan mortgages, know your banker's position, and have your documents ready, you're now ready to approach your local SBA office to present your case. In order to do justice to the SBA and the hundreds of small businessmen who have been helped by this agency, I can appropriately end this chapter with the visit of Charlie Anderson to his local SBA office—and his successful attempt to get an SBA loan.

Charlie Anderson owns a barge line on a midwestern river. He is a small operator and has some pretty big competitors, with fixed assets of millions of dollars. Competition in the barge business is brutal; all barge lines, big and small, have to meet competition from the railroads, trucking lines, as well as intra-mode competition.

Charlie was doing a good business, but it wasn't growing. He found that he needed additional equipment to provide better service for his existing clients, as well as for prospective customers who had heard about him.

Charlie went to the SBA office nearest his home. He was greeted pleasantly and asked to talk about his problems. He told the SBA that he was short of funds and needed $350,000.

"From the very first moment that I walked into the SBA office, there was evidence of a great desire to help," Charlie told me. "The top financial expert came in and talked over my problem with me. I explained the need for additional equipment and capital, and the competitiveness of our business. After reviewing the papers, the financial expert made suggestions as to how I might tighten up the operation internally. These suggestions paid off almost immediately. I was able to save a great deal of money by following these suggestions, but was still in need of additional financing.

"Senator Proxmire, I should like to say that one of the finest aspects of the SBA loan program is the counseling that they give to people like me. These loan specialists and financial experts have a wealth of knowledge. Even had I not gotten financial assistance from SBA, I would be grateful for everything they did for me."

But Charlie went back to the SBA office, said that additional money was needed, and was given a loan application. He talked with his local banker, who agreed to participate in the $300,000 loan to the extent of 25 per cent—$75,000.

The loan application was submitted to the local SBA office and, after the SBA appraiser had taken a look at the company assets, Charlie got his loan.

6

THE NEW CONGRESSIONAL EFFORT:
ITS SUCCESS AND FAILURE

Three brothers started a small manufacturing business in northern Wisconsin with initial capital of five dollars. After a promising beginning making bamboo fishing rods, they were all but wiped out when fiberglass became the preferred material for rods.

This small concern might have become just another statistic in the business-failure column. Instead, with the help of $250,000 and some sound management advice from a new kind of institution, the Small Business Investment Company, the firm now employs about 300 people in what has been classed as a labor distressed area.

Al Ruvelson, a dynamic and brilliant business expert, is the guiding genius of First Midwest Capital Corporation, the small business investment company that made this success possible—and, more importantly, provided the advice that put this small manufacturer on the road to success. Al's investment and advice company is the product of a law I co-sponsored, which passed the Congress in 1958.

As conceived by Congress, small business investment companies were to become a fourth banking system, designed specifically to fill the equity gap described in Chapter 3. Standing beside commercial banks, investment banks, and mortgage lending facilities, they were to become special agencies to serve the needs of small business which had nowhere else to turn for long-term loans.

I say "were to become" because the SBICs, as I will show later on in this chapter, have not fulfilled the bright promise they seemed to hold back in 1958.

Let us first turn to the positive side of the SBIC story. The new SBIC companies, privately organized, privately financed, and privately managed, are licensed by the Small Business Administration and must operate under ground rules laid out by it.

In addition, an SBIC may qualify for certain government benefits in order to attract private investment dollars into the financing of small business, which, admittedly, involves some risks. For example, the Small Business Administration may help finance an SBIC by lending it money. The Internal Revenue Code has been amended to give special treatment to investors who have lost money in an SBIC.

In return for these benefits, SBICs—at least as Congress originally conceived them—are restricted in what they can do. For one thing, they are supposed to finance only eligible small business. They can make long-term loans or equity investments, thus they are precluded from competition with most other financing institutions. Since the minimum term of SBIC loans is five years, such financing obviously runs longer than the term loans of the banks.

But there are also other differences. SBICs are aiming primarily at capital appreciation through the growth of the businesses they help; thus they usually seek an equity interest in the borrower.

Secondly, the SBICs usually work closely with the management of the small business, giving financial counsel and other assistance as requested and required. They provide this follow-through service since they are established by law to give management aid as well as financial assistance, and because they have a vested interest in the sound and steady growth of the borrower.

One of the witnesses who appeared before Congress during the 1963 hearings on the SBIC was a retail grocer from North Carolina. He needed a long-term loan so that he could buy store fixtures and make other improvements to compete with the large food chains. After he received $21,000—and management advice— from an SBIC in his locality, he was able to increase his volume and his profits. He testified that there was no other place for him to go for such a loan.

In California, an independent, intrastate airline needed capital to enable it to purchase some modern aircraft. At that time, private funds were not available and the airline could not tap the public market. An

SBIC's investment put four new planes in the air, buttressing the airline's financial position and enabling it to raise additional capital through private sources eighteen months later.

In mid-1963, there were over 650 SBICs in operation in almost every state and in a number of territories. One SBIC deals primarily with Eskimos in Alaska; others finance local business in Guam and the Virgin Islands.

These 650 SBICs have extended money and counsel to an estimated eight or nine thousand firms, from the smallest retailer to firms employing several hundred people.

In 1962, the late President Kennedy told the SBIC industry that its success so far "has been encouraging and confirms my confidence in its value. I believe [it] has great potential as a fourth banking system to fill the long-term and equity capital needs of small business."

Individual SBICs present a vast range of resources. The majority of them have the capital minimum of $300,000, and thus can lend no more than $60,000 to any one business. From this point, SBICs' resources range to that of the largest SBIC, which has private capital of about $35 million. By the time the SBIC program had reached its fifth anniversary in August, 1963, it had amassed capital of almost $600 million. Since they can also borrow approximately $250 million from the Small Business Administration, the program's total resources for helping small business had then reached $850 million.

So far, I have sketched the success side of the SBIC story—a side worth telling about. The SBICs without doubt have given many a small businessman the capital and advice he needed, and couldn't get anywhere else. But there is another, negative side to the story, presenting the sad spectacle of an instrumentality set up to benefit small business being used more and more to help financiers and investors make money.

The fact is that too great a percentage of SBIC funds are going—through an administrative misinterpretation of the SBIC act, as amended in 1961—to medium-size and even to "small" big businesses.

The clear congressional intent was that the SBICs, with their rich tax privileges and other advantages, not make investments exceeding $500,000 without the written approval of SBA. And that approval, in my judgment, should be exceptional. This $500,000 loan limitation was adopted as my amendment, supplementing the existing loan size limitation of 20 per cent of the capital surplus of an SBIC.

Then what happened? The SBA decided that the Proxmire amendment meant that the $500,000 loan ceiling need be applied only to 50 per cent of an SBIC's funds. The SBA interpretation states that an SBIC can escape the $500,000 limitation that Congress imposed half of the time, providing that it abides by the limitation the other half of the time.

This interpretation makes no sense to me. It is as though a legislative body were to pass a law against murder, and then issue the "interpretation" that one could commit murder every other day, or on odd days.

In practice, this interpretive ruling means that the very rich and substantial tax advantages given under the law to SBICs, providing them in effect with a form of subsidized capital, are in some instances not being used for the benefit of small business. Instead, large amounts of money are going to firms which can be classified as "small business" only by stretching the definition to laughable lengths.

Item: Boston Capital Corporation, an SBIC, invested $780,000 in Research Specialties Company, a publicly held company whose stock is available to the public. This company is not held by a family or by a few individuals, which might mean difficulties in its raising funds privately. The market value of the $780,000 investment rose in a few months to $1,426,000.

Item: Business Funds, Inc., an SBIC, invested $800,-000 in Allvac Metals of North Carolina, a publicly held company. This company produces high temperature and special alloys, and its sales were over $1 million during the first half of 1961. The SBIC's net profit for the six-month period was $163,000.

Item: Business Funds, Inc. also invested $1.5 million in Unanco Corporation, a national construction firm based in California. In 1962 it was estimated that Unanco would do $35 million worth of business.

Item: Electronics Capital Corporation of San Diego, an SBIC, invested $750,000 in the Potter Instrument Co. Within a few months, the market value of this investment increased to $9,300,000. The value of Potter Instrument at that time was some $30 million, and Electronics Capital had a 30.8 per cent equity in it.

The terms "small business" and "small business investment company" hardly seem to apply to such undertakings as those preceding. Certainly it is wonderful that people can make this kind of profit investing in large businesses, but I submit that these businesses should not be subsidized in the name of small business.

The Proxmire amendment of 1961, limiting investments to $500,000, was to prevent exactly this type of investment and to make sure that SBIC funds would assist genuine small businesses, the kind which, because of their size and needs, have the hardest time getting equity financing.

It is plain that large SBICs are putting more and more of their investment money into big loans. What makes this development particularly serious is that new rules and regulations are being promulgated which have the effect of restricting the formation of new, small SBICs. It is going to become more difficult to obtain a license at the minimum capital level of $150,-000. Yet these smaller SBICs are the ones which make the loans to small businesses.

The SBIC program has a great potential—if it can

get back on the track and become what Congress intended. At this writing, many SBICs are helping firms that do not genuinely need this kind of assistance; on the other hand, a large number of small businesses that could use this capital are not getting it.

I have seen projections of a study, showing that there will be literally thousands of loans and investments made by SBICs to small businesses. I earnestly hope that this is true. And as chairman of the Subcommittee on Small Business of the Banking and Currency Committee, I intend to do all I can to make sure this happens.

7

WHY NOT LET THE LOCAL
BOYS HELP?

You have put your skills and your creativity into high gear to make your business a success. Your money is tied up in it as well. Yet you know your business has not reached its potential. But because you have faith in your business and confidence that the buying public needs your product, you want to expand.

You need long-term financing to tide you over the expansion, but the bank in your community would rather make short-term, sure-thing loans, and considers your venture on the risky side.

Or maybe yours is a new, untried business, one that presents an even greater picture of risk to the bank. You're willing to sink all you can into it, but the banks just aren't interested enough.

If you're a good risk, if your ideas are sound, if you need long-term capital because you're new or expanding but you're having plenty of trouble convincing your bank, why not let the local boys help? Or if you're on the move, let the boys in the next county or in another state know about it.

There are more than 14,000 industrial development groups throughout the country and they are eager to help you, because your industry can help them by building a greater economic base in the communities they represent. Basically their purpose is to attract you to their towns. And competition between them to win you is keen. Some will even come to you if you can't go to them.

They will put their best foot forward, telling you about the availability of labor, manufacturing materials, and transportation as well as about the market for your product. Some have brochures that will give you details about their town's water and power supply. Some may sell or give you land that has been made ready for industrial occupancy. Others may give, lease, or sell you a building, tell you about the tax concessions or the favorable tax climate in their town, talk to the local bank to get you the loan you need, or even lend you the money themselves.

This is the case in Elkhorn, Wisconsin, a town that lives by its motto: "A Progressive City With a Future."

Despite its small population of 3,586, since 1939 Elkhorn has been thinking big in terms of industrial development. In that year, voters approved a referendum allowing the city council to appropriate $2,000 per year to encourage and assist new industry in locating in Elkhorn.

Nothing happened for six years. But in 1945, when

the first nibble of interest came from industry, the city council created an independent body to administer an industrial expansion program—the Elkhorn Development Company, Inc.

This municipally owned, non-profit body uses city funds to attract new firms to Elkhorn by buying land ahead of time, and by financing that portion of the building for which an industry is unable to obtain a bank loan, and cannot itself pay.

One such industry is owned by Mr. and Mrs. Victor G. Fiegel, who moved the A.K. Rubber Products Company to Elkhorn because they were unable to get financial help in their own village. Waiting for them was a $1,500 parcel of land with plenty of room for expansion, which the Elkhorn Development Company was eager to sell them.

Needing $30,000 to build their plant, the Fiegels received a $12,500 loan from the First National Bank of Elkhorn and a $7,500 loan from the Elkhorn Development Company. They already had $11,500 of their own. Although they opened the plant with only two employees, the Fiegels now have thirteen permanent employees and sometimes hire up to twenty.

The story of the Fiegel's expansion parallels Elkhorn's own industrial expansion. It now has seventeen industries which were not there in 1945. The smallest employs four men and the largest more than 1,000 persons. The most recent land acquisition by the development company, a 230-acre farm within the city limits, is for a new industrial park. The cost to the city and to the local taxpayers is still $2,000 per year, a cost they can better afford today because of the bigger tax base.

In Wisconsin, there are approximately 220 privately organized local development corporations, in which the butcher, baker, and barber have a cash interest. Generally, these corporations operate by selling stock and debentures to finance construction of plants for lease to industry. Wisconsin's Department of Resource Development feels local development corporations have worked especially well in its state. Wisconsin is proud of the local private initiative these self-help companies represent.

While local development groups work on selling their immediate communities to industry, many states, through development authorities or corporations, have taken on the job of selling their state by helping to finance new or expanding industry.

These state corporations, created by state law, permit individual states to lend money, either directly to industry or to local development corporations.

Although all development groups do not operate the same way, their aims are similar; maintenance and growth of the economic base of the state or community by strengthening its tax and job base. Some local groups are run for profit, some are not. Some sell stock and operate from private funds, while others use funds from the sale of municipal bonds. Some were formed exclusively to benefit from low-term government financing programs, while others use only their own funds. Some borrow from their big brothers, the state development corporations. Some are strictly promotion groups, which function mainly as their towns' industrial welcoming committees, making sure that new or expanding business knows it is wanted by their communities.

Paradoxically, even though the purpose of industrial expansion is to build a better community through a bigger tax base, some states and towns will lose taxes to win industry. This sometimes amounts to giving one business a competitive advantage over another.

In some cases, states and municipalities will give five or ten year property tax-free inducement to new businesses. During these years, a company will not be paying for municipal roads, water systems, schools, and airports. The tax burden then falls on home owners, or on the established home business, which has never been given the same break. The public facilities the new business needs for the purpose of operating are paid for by others.

Similarly, a municipal development company is guilty of reducing the tax base when it leases a plant to a business, since neither the industry nor the development company pays taxes on the property to the community. Incidentally, the industry's rent can be deducted as a business expense from federal income tax, providing a further tax benefit to the industry.

Uncle Sam has been aware of this problem for some time, and may some day take action to prevent such tax advantages. For it can be argued that it is chiefly labor, market, and raw materials—not tax advantages—that determine the location of an industry, and that tax advantages merely become a windfall to industry while the community gets robbed of tax dollars for public facility growth; perhaps the industry would have chosen the same community regardless of tax benefits. It is evident also that if a town does not receive the maximum tax benefit from every possible source, this may cause a lag in the construction of the very public facilities it needs to maintain and attract business.

Meanwhile, Uncle Sam will continue to work hard on programs which help development corporations, such as the one offered by the Small Business Administration. If you cannot get full financing from a bank, the SBA will make loans to both state and local development companies for specific businesses planning plant construction, modernization, or expansion. The funds may be used for the purchase of land, machinery, or equipment. In most cases there is some bank participation in the program.

Your state or local development company may then borrow up to $350,000 on a single loan for you, and the federal government only asks 5.5 per cent interest per annum. If a participating bank sets a lower rate of interest, the SBA will make its rate the same, but not lower than 5 per cent per annum. And the development company can take up to twenty-five years to pay the government back. The SBA will not make a development company loan for a relocating business, however, unless it is clearly shown that the business needs to move closer to raw materials or to the market, to consolidate operations in one location, or the like.

The SBA program solely for state development companies differs from the one above in that the federal loan matches loans obtained from banks and other private sources, and need not be for specific businesses. A loan to a certain business is limited to the amount the business owes on borrowings from other sources. Of course, the state development company must have funds of its own to invest in or to lend to small business, along with the SBA funds, and the minimum state participation in a loan is at least one-third as much as the SBA provides. Interest under this program is 5 per cent, with a period of twenty years for repayment.

Another government program, for large or small business, is the depressed areas program. Low-term industrial loans, loans and grants for such facilities as sewer and water mains, roads, railroad spurs, and underwritten technical studies, are available if the federal investment of funds will create permanent jobs in areas where mass unemployment and underemployment exist. Grants to train skilled labor also are available under this program.

The federal agency administering the depressed areas program, the Area Redevelopment Administration, assists only new businesses or businesses that are expanding, so as not to pirate industry from or cause unemployment in economically healthy areas.

71

The ARA may lend up to 65 per cent of the cost of a new or expanding plant at 4 per cent interest. Loans may be made directly to private business, public non-profit groups, development corporations, or government bodies. Loan recipients may take up to twenty-five years to repay.

Under the SBA program for areas in economic distress, loans may be made to state or local development companies at a rate of 4 per cent interest, for businesses in depressed areas or in areas of substantial unemployment, as designated by the Labor Department. Under the program solely for state development companies, the SBA likewise will reduce its interest rate to 4 per cent, provided the loan is given to a firm situated in a depressed area or in an area of substantial unemployment.

Can You Remedy
Management Weakness?

8
IS SOUND BUSINESS TRAINING
AVAILABLE?

What I'll call "Jensen Cheese" is a household word in Wisconsin. And since young Jack Jensen inherited the family business and began shipping cheese under a supermarket contract he landed, the chances are that you've seen Jensen Gouda and other Wisconsin specialties on the party food shelves of your local supermarket branch.

With the supermarket deal, Jack's business began growing spectacularly in 1960 and 1961. As it grew, Jack found that there was more to do than he could manage himself. When he attempted to delegate some phase of his management operation to another, however, he noticed a resentment on the part of other employees toward the selected person. Indeed, ironing out petty differences among his staff began to take up a large part of his time.

Jack discussed his problems with a fellow businessman, who told him that the state university, in cooperation with the Small Business Administration, was beginning a course in factory management and personnel problems.

At first Jack was skeptical. He didn't like the idea of going back to school, so he talked himself into believing that he was too busy and that the course would be a waste of time. "What do these people know about the cheese business?" he asked himself.

But after a key employee with thirty-five years at Jensen Cheese walked out in a rage, Jack decided he had better try to get help somewhere. The SBA "school" might at least be a start even though it couldn't possibly—so he thought—get down to cases so far as his own business was concerned.

Jack's first surmise was correct. There wasn't much the SBA could tell him about making cheese. But he was amazed to learn that Jensen Cheese was far from unique in its management and personnel problems. No matter what their line of business, his fellow students were experiencing the same kind of difficulties and irritations as he was in his own employee relations.

Moreover, several other businessmen who were going through the tensions and adjustments of business expansion had also lost valuable employees through petty misunderstandings. As discussions revealed the large area of common experience, Jack entered enthusiastically into the course. He decided that it was going to be very practical indeed—not all high-flown theory as he had feared.

Jack learned that he should have a pattern in delegating work. He was told that if he gave each employee

a certain specialized area in which to exercise responsibility, there would be less jealousy when new assign-
ments were made. He also learned that the quality of
work would improve as the employee became more familiar with his own area of responsibility.

Jack enjoyed the classes and lost no time in putting
into effect what he had been taught. His problems were
not solved immediately, but in a short time he could
tell that they were being alleviated. He is now a firm
supporter of management courses.

There was never a time in our history when competition among business concerns has been keener than it
is today. The time has passed when an easygoing ama-
teur could, with a little bit of luck, make the grade.
There is no place in today's business world for medi-
ocrity. To succeed you have to be a shrewd manager—
a "pro" in every sense of the word.

Although professional standards are needed for success in the professions, none are required of you by any
outside authority before you enter business. Before one
can enter into the practice of law or medicine, he has
to meet exacting standards of skill. In his practice, he
has to live up to strict standards of conduct and ethics.
Business, however, is different. One can go into business without meeting professional standards of efficiency and skill, and in business there are no generally
recognized standards of ethics or conduct.

This lack of business standards and the poor management practices that result have been the cause of many
business failures, tragic wastes of human and financial

resources. The problem is clear. What can we do about it?

We will not lessen the large number of business failures by restricting severely the right of a person to enter business. Freedom to go into business should be jealously guarded. What is needed is a more adequate training program for young people who plan to make business a career. For those already in business, specialized as well as general educational opportunities should be expanded.

The need for a better business education program has been a subject of growing interest among educators, businessmen, and the government.

Most businessmen in the United States have never attended a business school. Of course, business education does not automatically guarantee a successful career in business. It is, however, becoming increasingly important.

The most dramatic examples of the results of specialized management training are the outstanding careers of the ten young men—the "Whiz Kids"—who joined the Ford Motor Company shortly after World War II. All of these men had studied business administration at the graduate level.

The most widely known and the leader of the group was Robert S. McNamara, who, after being with Ford for fourteen years, was elected president in 1960. On January 3, 1961, he was appointed Secretary of Defense by President Kennedy. Another member of the group was Arjay Miller, the current president of the Ford

Motor Company. Of the original ten one is deceased, and the other seven have important positions with Ford or are highly successful in their own businesses.

Of course, plenty of top executives didn't go to business school. M. J. Rathbone, president and chief executive officer of the Standard Oil Company of New Jersey, is a graduate chemical engineer. Zach Toms, president of Liggett and Myers Tobacco Company, joined the company while he was still a student at the University of Virginia, where he majored in classical languages. Thus there is no educational pattern we can use to determine whether or not a man will be a success in business. The human factor remains the most important element.

Nevertheless, I firmly believe in the utility of high-grade business education. Day-to-day business operations are growing more complex, and the training needed to aid the businessman in making wise decisions can be provided in part by our schools of business. As business education techniques improve, this part of a businessman's training becomes more valuable. Business schools are, therefore, getting more attention from our educators.

The administrators of schools and departments of business have known for some time that there was a need for a reappraisal of business school education in this country. The state of collegiate business schools was very closely examined by two 1959 studies. One, sponsored by the Carnegie Corporation of New York, was *The Education of American Businessmen,* by Frank C.

Pierson. The other, *Higher Education for Business,* by Robert A. Gordon and James E. Howell, was sponsored by the Ford Foundation.

These studies were very critical of the present state of business education, and recommended many changes. They found a lack of professional standards in schools of business, incompetent professors, low salaries, poor planning of courses, and inferior students. They recommended that professional standards be set, that the number of courses be reduced and their scope broadened, and that both professors and students be upgraded in the schools.

The Carnegie and Ford studies also indicated that too many collegiate schools of business have been concentrating on a vocational type of training at the expense of the liberal arts. They pointed out that this training might be acceptable in preparing the student for his first job, but it would be of no value in training him for the continuous growth that will be demanded of him in his business career.

As a result of these studies, there is a growing trend in liberal arts colleges to provide a broader educational background for professional business administrators. There is recognition that business education should not only prepare a person for a career in business, but should lay the foundation for continuous learning on his part. It should train him to adapt to various changes over the long period of his business life, as well as give him the resources for continuous personal growth in areas other than business. If he develops all his human potentials, he will be a better and more successful businessman.

The particular needs of the small businessman and the specialized character of some industries have been used to justify narrow business training. The small businessman needs a very broad background, however, since he will not be able to afford the help of specialists. Moreover, he has the same need to develop his human potentials outside of his business role as the corporation executive if he is to live a full and meaningful life.

Various types of schools offer regular courses in the broad field of business. These courses are available on a full-time basis to students just finishing high school, on a part-time basis to students who work, and to business executives in all stages of their careers. The first and most important of these schools are the collegiate schools of business.

In the late 1800's, there were only three organized schools of business; today there are about 160. In addition, formal degree programs in business are now offered by more than 400 college departments or divisions not organized as separate schools. One out of every seven degrees awarded by institutions of higher education in the United States is in business administration. The number of degrees awarded in this field is second only to the number in the field of education.

Graduate work in business has increased greatly since World War II. In 1939–1940, when I received my master's degree in business administration, graduate business education accounted for only 2 per cent of all master's degrees. By 1957–1958, the share of graduate business education had risen to 7 per cent. Only a small number of students (2.8 per cent) obtained their doctor's degree in business, however.

The demand by practicing businessmen for further educational help has increased greatly since World War II. This has resulted in a very rapid growth—both in the number of courses and the number of students—of evening and extension business education programs offered by colleges and universities. In fact, the number who seek part-time or postgraduate education exceeds the number of regular students in business schools. It has been estimated that each year approximately 225,-000 adults take at least one credit course in evening colleges or university extension divisions in some phase of business education. These programs vary from conferences lasting only a few hours to programs leading to a degree.

Management courses for small businessmen, sponsored by the Small Business Administration and colleges, universities, and local groups, are becoming better known. During 1963, 551 of these courses were held in 275 educational institutions throughout the country. This represents an increase of nearly 24 per cent in attendance, and of nearly 20 per cent in the number of courses conducted over 1962. These courses cover such subjects as tax and legal problems, management records, U.S. government contract administration, planning, office management, human relations, sales management, and marketing. Usually they are conducted once a week during the evening hours, and generally run for an eight to ten-week period.

The Vocational Education and the Distributive Education Divisions of the U.S. Department of Health, Education, and Welfare also sponsor management courses for small businessmen. Many of the courses are supported by state and local education agencies, and local chambers of commerce.

Educational opportunities are not offered by the government alone. Corporations, as well as local groups, also are interested in increasing the knowledge of our present and future businessmen.

Even with the variety of schools available, many small businessmen do not take advantage of them. While some do not have the time or the money to attend, the steady increase in enrollment statistics shows that businessmen are rapidly finding out how valuable these schools can be, and are making special efforts to attend.

There is no real agreement as to what or how much should be taught in order to provide the best education for business. But at least attempts are being made to find out. Much still needs to be done in the realm of business education. The quality of schools has to be improved, teaching standards have to be raised, and more publicity is needed to explain the necessity for and the benefits of business training. While our whole educational system could be strengthened by the same improvements, they are particularly needed by our business schools, in which education is so closely related to practical goals.

Education can make success come more quickly and make life more rewarding to both the individual and society. However, even with the best schools and teachers, the real secret of success in business lies with the student.

9
CAN YOU HIRE THE TECHNICAL BRAINS?

In business, brains are a product always in short supply. Brains and talent, of course, are useful in the most simple small business operation. They can be the lifeblood of your company if you are operating one of the more complex small electronics or manufacturing firms.

Take the case of Pittsylvania Tool. Pittsylvania, founded in the owner's basement in 1937 on $1,000 capital, was a going business, employing thirty people, when it was purchased by two men who did not understand its technical manufacturing processes. These men, furthermore, did not exercise enough care and judgment in hiring a new plant manager.

Pittsylvania, at the time of the purchase, had received a government contract for $120,000 worth of gun parts, which had to be manufactured to close tolerance. The contracted work was so bad under the new manager, however, that the whole order was rejected by the government. Finally, the new owners called in the former owner—manager and asked him to reorganize the manufacturing operation. But all the money spent on the contract was lost, and it was too late to bail the company out. Bankruptcy followed.

Perhaps when you started your company you could easily handle the whole business yourself. You could be both the businessman and the technician. You could keep the books, make the sales, run the machines, and make the deliveries.

As your business has improved and new orders have begun to come in, you've probably found that you are no longer able to operate your business alone. New technical advances require that you buy new and more complicated machines in order to compete. And you simply don't have the time to perform well all the administrative tasks your expanding business requires. Maybe you find yourself neglecting to check out bills for supplies and material as carefully as you once did, or doing the bookkeeping a month late, or letting orders lie around for a week without proper acknowledgment.

If this is the case, you have definitely reached a stage in your development where you need competent help in order to keep your business alive and growing. You need technical brains. And as I've already indicated, an employee who can and will keep cost, sales, and advertising records—and help you use them with imagination —is worth his weight in gold.

Last year, the Department of Commerce reported that there were 155,000 electronic, mechanical, and aeronautical engineers, and 175,000 positions for them. This means a nationwide shortage of 20,000 engineers. There is also a shortage of adequately trained technicians below the level of engineer, and of trained cost accountants.

These shortages have resulted in sharp competition for specialized talent. It will take great ingenuity on your part to select the man (or men) you need for your business and keep him.

This shortage will, of course, put you in competition not only with other small businesses but with larger firms as well. These large firms will have money to spend on attractive and well-planned recruitment drives. They will stress the advantages of working for a big concern. There will be an elaborate presentation of their fringe benefits, such as vacations, insurance, retirement, and so on. They will emphasize that they can offer the best and most modern equipment. They will stress the unlimited possibilities of advancement that only a big concern can offer.

Some of their claims may be valid. It is true that large firms offer fringe benefits that you will not be able to match. The prestige alone of some big firm names will, no doubt, attract many of the better young men. The glamor of big contracts and the opportunity to participate in them will attract others.

It will be up to you to meet these claims with a clear presentation of the many benefits of working for a small firm. Impress on your prospective employee that he will have the opportunity to grow with your company, that he will have a chance to be in close touch with top management, and be "on the inside" in management decisions. Stress that he will be able to make wider use of his talents in a small firm, that he will not be made to specialize as he might in a large firm. Sell the point that many of the vital scientific advances of our age have come from small research firms, and that many interesting and challenging contracts for scientific development are awarded to small firms. Convey to him a sense of your own interest in what your firm does. Also, an ownership percentage may attract a key employee.

There are several things that you must consider before you go out into the market in search of your man. What kind of training or experience will you require of your new employee? Are you prepared and able to train a new college graduate in the work that you will require, or will you need an experienced man who can fit immediately into your operation?

You must exercise extreme caution in choosing your man. You must have the objectives of your business, as well as its potentialities and limitations, firmly in mind. Initiative to help plan policy put into the wrong hands can be worse than no extra hands at all.

Take the case of the Midtown Foundry, a small plant with built-in diversification because of its large stock of machine tools, added by the versatile manager over the years. The business depnded mainly on job foundry work, and operations could be changed quickly by moving tools in and out of the production line.

Midtown's owner, Mickey Snyder, was pretty well satisfied with his business, which had an area-wide reputation for high-grade work. When the operations became too much for him to handle alone, he hired a young engineer whose specialty was (so he said) steel. The chance at a large contract to produce ingot steel (about which Mickey knew next to nothing) proved most enticing. Mickey had his doubts, but allowed his new engineer to talk him into signing. Job foundry work was neglected in the attempt to convert to the exacting production of the special steel.

The venture, as you can probably guess, proved disastrous. Neither Mickey nor his new employee possessed the high degree of skill needed for the open hearth furnace process; the specialized knowledge of Mickey's bright young man proved to be merely theoretical. Two old reconverted furnaces and two new ones never produced salable ingots, and in six months Mickey lost his business.

When you have clearly in mind what kind of man you want and what you have to offer, you can begin your recruitment campaign. You should be aware of the services that are available to you in your recruitment effort. Trade associations, the U.S. Employment Service in your state, and the Small Business Administration are equipped to give you assistance, but you may have to go to some trouble and effort to secure it. There may not be an office of the Small Business Administration or of the employment office in your town. The services they have to offer, however, are valuable enough to you to make a visit to the nearest office worthwhile, and since they are free, your efforts to take advantage of them will mean only an investment of time.

You may find that engineers and technicians can be secured by recommendation from your own employees. Do not try to handle employee recruitment by mail or telephone.

I should warn you that other methods of recruitment of competent technical personnel can be expensive. It has been estimated that it costs between $3,000 and $5,000 to recruit one really capable engineer. This figure is, of course, out of the reach of most small businessmen. You will have to exercise judgment in seeing that your money is well spent.

You will find that the college placement method will not only cost you the money it takes to visit various colleges, but also the valuable time needed for effective interviews and follow-ups. Classified advertisements, if they set out in detail the qualifications required and are run for a considerable period of time in various publications, also can be expensive.

There is a growing tendency among engineers, technicians, and other specialists to seek employment in small firms. The image of the organization man of the large corporation is distasteful to them. They feel that the sense of individual accomplishment can best be satisfied in the atmosphere of the small, rather than large concern.

These are very real factors in your favor when you search for the services of bright young men for your company. Don't be apologetic or hestitant about bringing them to the attention of those you seek to recruit.

10

WHAT ABOUT ADVICE FROM UNCLE SAM'S EXPERTS?

Don Dunnington runs a small appliance shop in Baraboo, Wisconsin. He has built a fine reputation on his good selection of products and his efficient repair service.

Not content to stand still, however, Don decided to seek financing in order to expand his inventory and modernize his showroom. But unlike many small businessmen who feel they are the only ones who can possibly understand their own operations, Don wanted some advice on the steps he was going to take.

He spent months talking to many experts in the area: bankers, local lenders, and others. Finally, feeling that he was not getting anywhere, Don wrote me, asking about various federal agencies which give advice and help to businessmen.

"Is there any way I can take advantage of this without coming to Washington?" he asked. "And is there any agency which will bother about a small shop like mine?" I advised Don to approach the Madison branch office of the Small Business Administration, not only as to his need for a loan but to get an expert opinion on his proposed expansion program.

Don wrote me again to tell me that he had visited the Madison SBA office, where he "received more valuable advice than all during the past year and a half" from other sources.

"I was very gratified with the reception and counseling I got," Don's letter continued, "even though I was not able to obtain any financial help.

"When I left the meeting in Madison I had an entirely different view as far as the finances and my own particular business are concerned. Lawrence Hayes and the other men I talked with pointed out several different approaches to my problems. By working along these lines I have been able to obtain my financing locally and am now in the best position I have ever been since I went into business."

Unfortunately, relatively few businessmen seek advice so aggressively and have open enough minds to profit so dramatically from it. This is a great misfortune, because today much good advice is available from both government and private sources—advice which you usually obtain either free or for a nominal fee. Small businessmen in particular ought to take advantage of it.

Dun and Bradstreet, Inc., one of the largest compilers of business statistics in the country, alleges that 91.3

per cent of business failures lies in management weakness. They have classified these weaknesses as: (1) Lack of experience in the business, accounting for 9.8 per cent of the failures in 1961; (2) lack of managerial experience, accounting for 17.2 per cent; (3) unbalanced experience by management, accounting for 19.9 per cent; and (4) incompetence, accounting for 44.4 per cent. This last category includes businessmen and women who do not have the ability to plan, to manage, or to control. They lack the basic intellectual ability or self-discipline needed to operate a business successfully. They do not listen to advice or profit from error.

This survey clearly points to the vital need of the small business community for management advice, since an overwhelming percentage of the failures are among small businesses.

It is interesting to note, however, that recently Dun and Bradstreet made a survey of the need of small businesses for counsel, interviewing 1,000 small businessmen. While 47 per cent did not believe they needed help, the remaining 53 per cent said that they go for advice to people they do business with—suppliers, banks, accountants, and lawyers. They also go to their trade associations and the government.

This proven need of small business for management help and counsel has intensified efforts of both public and private organizations to provide advice. The federal government is rapidly increasing its counseling facilities.

The Small Business Administration

The Small Business Act of 1958 authorizes the Small Business Administration to "provide . . . managerial aids to small business concerns, by advising and counseling . . . on policies, principles, and practices of good management. . . ."

Under this authority, the Small Business Administration has instituted several programs designed to help you solve your management problems. Of these, the management publications program is the most widely used. SBA publications are directed to people who already are in business or who intend to start one. They are directed to all types of business—retail, wholesale, manufacturing, service, and others—and they provide information on a variety of subjects, including meeting competition, exporting, business insurance, sales, legal structure, depreciation, and quality control. Since the beginning of the program, some 450 titles have been published, and as of March 31, 1962, more than 3.8 million copies of these publications had been distributed.

The Small Business Administration also has a contract research program, through which it makes contract arrangements with experts or companies to conduct specialized studies of small business problems. It also has the authority, under the Small Business Act, to grant up to $40,000 per year to states, universities, and other agencies in order to help pay for studies concerning the management, financing, and operation of small business concerns.

The SBA received appropriations for this program in 1959 and 1960, but it has been unable to secure appropriations from Congress since 1960 to continue the program. This is partly because a lot of the original grant money was not wisely spent, being wasted—in my opinion—on investigation of "fringe" business ventures. Still, many of these research studies are valuable sources of basic data, which are available nowhere else. If you'd like to check to see if your own industry or business has been the subject of a study, you may send to SBA for a list of the reports completed to date.

As I mentioned in Chapter 8, the Small Business Administration conducts, in cooperation with various educational institutions, administrative management courses. These courses have grown in acceptance through the years, and as of June, 1962, 1,560 had been held, co-sponsored by 508 different educational institutions, and with an enrollment of over 47,000 small business owners and managers.

SBA also supplements these courses with management conferences, usually one-day meetings on subjects of interest to a wide range of owners and managers of small business concerns.

Finally, as in the case of Don Dunnington, the SBA tries to counsel those who bring their problems to its regional offices. Often—as in Don's case, and in the case of Charlie Anderson, the barge-line owner—this counsel can be as valuable as an outright loan.

The SBA is limited in its ability to offer individual counsel to small businessmen, however, because of lack of personnel. In three of its regional offices, SBA has only two management consultants, while the other twelve have only one. This means that, in the case of Chicago, for example, there is only one consultant to serve the interests of an estimated 100,000 small businesses!

The Department of Commerce

Another fine source of management assistance is the U.S. Department of Commerce. Unfortunately this agency, while aware that small business predominates numerically on the American scene, always has opposed any sharp distinction between small and big business. For this reason many of its services and publications will have to be used selectively.

In the first few months of the Kennedy administration, Commerce went through a top-to-bottom shake-up, and recently a second reorganization has taken place. The agency today reflects a new belief that home and overseas markets are becoming more and more similar, and that the problems of dealing with each market ought not to be separated. The Business and Defense Services Administration has been regrouped into seven "commodity" or "industry" divisions, which not only gather information and statistics on domestic business but cooperate with the overseas division of Commerce as well. The latter division now is called the Bureau of International Commerce; the many valuable services it offers to the small businessman interested in export will be described in detail in Chapter 18.

Besides these reorganization dislocations, the Commerce Department has been plagued by the difficulties of managing the hodge-podge of agencies it has acquired through the years—some of them in "raids" on other executive agencies. Among its other activities, Commerce weighs and measures (through the National Bureau of Standards), keeps an eye on the weather (through the U.S. Weather Bureau), counts heads (through the Census Bureau), and guards the brain children of inventors (through the Patent Office).

Most of these bureaus do contribute a wealth of statistics and data which help Commerce perform its main function: to assist you, the businessman, through publications and advisory services available directly through it, or through the thirty-four field offices located in major cities throughout the U.S.

Just how do you, a druggist in Kokomo or a grocery store owner in Iowa City, go about getting advice and assistance from Commerce? First of all, there are the department's many publications. Commerce publishes literally tons of material of interest to businessmen in general, and much of it will be valuable to you as a small businessman. Commerce is actually the largest publisher in the government.

Even more extensive than the publications of the SBA, Commerce's informational booklets and brochures on wholesaling, retailing, the service trades, technical processes, manufacturing, and marketing will be of special interest to you. If you come to Washington, be sure to visit the bookshop in Commerce's main lobby. Here are gathered most of the business publications put out by all departments of the government. The books and pamphlets are arranged by subject, and there is someone to help you place your order and to give you suggestions on other sources of information.

A monthly *Marketing Information Guide*, to which you can subscribe, will bring listings of the material available from Commerce. You'll also be interested in the department's *Selected Publications,* a partial listing of its printed material. An annual subscription to the *Business Service Checklist* ($1.50 from the Government Printing Office), listing all Commerce publications of the week, is also valuable. The Department of Commerce also publishes an annotated listing of all its marketing and distribution aids, *Publications for Use in Marketing and Distribution.*

If you think you have a product the U.S. Government might be interested in buying, you can watch for your chance to bid by following the *Commerce Business Daily.* This newspaper lists government procurement invitations, subcontracting leads, contract awards, sales of surplus property, and foreign business opportunities. There is a special section in each issue listing those contracts which have been set aside exclusively for small business to bid on. Further information on the procedure for getting into federal procurement can be obtained from your local Commerce or SBA field office.

Even more helpful than the publications will be a

visit to the Commerce field office nearest you. The staff of this office can help you with advice on your business problems, drawing on the extensive data and statistical information gathered by the department on every aspect of business activity—marketing, distribution, manufacturing, production problems, and area development. Each field office also has a business reference library of periodicals, directories, publications, and reports that are of interest to businessmen—from private as well as government sources.

Finally, if you decide to bring your problems and dreams for the future to Washington, the department's "One-Stop Business Service Center" located off the main lobby of the Commerce building will be of special interest to you. This center has been set up to answer questions about the services and information offered to small businessmen by all U.S. government agencies. The information center has a trained staff that can analyze your own particular problems or locate people in government offices who can help you. They will even set up appointments for you to speak with these agency experts.

Commerce does—somewhat grudgingly—coordinate its activities with those of SBA. Because Commerce opposed the creation of SBA as a separate agency, wanting to keep all business affairs in its own hands, cooperation between the two agencies has never been enthusiastic. Therefore, if you come to Washington or if you plan to seek help on the regional level, your best bet would be to contact both agencies. Commerce has available a great deal of specialized and highly technical information which the SBA, with its limited staff, simply can't match.

For example, each year Commerce gathers some 100,000 research and development reports which represent non-classified government research. Some of this research may be pertinent to your business, and you may be able to make use of it to develop new products and to improve old ones. Large corporations have agents in Washington who are in touch regularly with Commerce, keeping up on the latest trends in government research and development. For a nominal fee, you too can benefit from the more than $10 billion per year Uncle Sam spends on research.

Commerce also maintains a vast file of technical information from all over the world (which it is currently readying for storage in a computer). Suppose you are like Charlie McQueen, who operates a small canning factory in Wisconsin. Charlie was having trouble with his beets: the flavor wasn't just right and people were complaining of a certain sour quality. When Charlie simply couldn't pin down the reason for this, he wrote me about it. My office got in touch with Commerce, and we sent a sample of Charlie's beets to the Technical Services Department.

For a small fee, technicians turned up 300 articles on beet processing—from all over the free world. Then Charlie's beets were sent to the Department of Agriculture for analysis. This provides a fine example of how the various executive agencies can work together.

The Department of Labor

Some of the services of the Department of Labor may also be of interest to you. First of all, there is the U.S. Employment Service, mentioned briefly in Chapter 9. Your state employment service—through its affiliation with the United States Employment Service—offers a number of related services to you, in addition to aid in the recruitment of personnel. For example, your state employment service can help you determine the basic requirements of the job you wish to create, interview and test prospective candidates, and, on request, help you analyze your own employment problems—particularly employee turnover.

Also the services of Labor's Bureau of Apprenticeship and Training can help you develop or improve apprentice programs in your own manufacturing or construction concern. Helping to set up apprenticeship programs in the construction, tool and die, and printing and publishing industries is the biggest part of the bureau's activities. Since most of the firms in these fields are small businesses, employing one to five trainees, the bureau's services can be very valuable. Such small firms obviously cannot employ a full-time training staff for their apprenticeship programs.

Take David Siegfreid, for example, the owner of a

six-employee machinery repair company in Philadelphia. Recently David got in touch with the regional Bureau of Apprenticeship office, seeking information on machinist training for two new employees. The employees were, of course, already working at their trade and were learning on the job. But there was little organization or curriculum; the trainee and the firm never really knew where the trainee stood in his development.

The Bureau helped Siegfreid secure training standards for machinist apprentices, and Siegfreid embarked on a formal apprenticeship program. One apprentice was registered as a start, and the young man's previous training and experience were evaluated so that he might receive credit. If his program works out, Siegfreid intends to enter other men as registered apprentices.

Another service—likely to be overlooked because its utility is not so evident—is available from the Bureau of Labor Statistics. A wealth of material has been published on such subjects as employment trends in various industries, wholesale and retail prices, work rates of different occupations by areas, and the like. In addition, the bureau will assemble data for you if statistics you need are not already published. Thus if you want to compare your plant or store record with similar enterprises in your locality or in your industry as a whole, you can get the figures you need from this bureau. If you're planning a branch in another part of town, or in a neighboring city, such information as this can be very useful.

Still other Department of Labor services are offered by the Bureau of Labor Standards and the Office of Manpower, Automation, and Training. From the former you can get help on your safety problems in the factory or shop; from the latter special programs of on-the-job training are being offered to individual employers under the Manpower Development and Training Act of 1962.

Other executive departments

Other executive departments also offer a variety of services and assistance. The Department of Interior, for example, maintains information and inquiries offices (and libraries) which can be useful to small businessmen concerned with public lands and parks, earth resources, water supply, and the like. In addition, the department has funds for loans and grants to small businesses in certain fields of exploration and research related to the earth and its resources. You can write to the Department of Interior, Washington 25, D.C., for the address of the field office (the department has more than 2,000) nearest you.

John Blake, for example, wanted to go into the tourist court business after his return from the army. He thought he would like to settle in Colorado. John first tried to get a concession for a tourist court in the Grand Smokey Park, but Interior turned him down. The department, however, through its National Park Service helped John survey the need for tourist courts in the general area of Grand Smokey Park, and he located a site outside the park area but near enough to serve the same tourists he would have accomodated had he been allowed to locate inside the park.

A fuller description of the services, assistance, and monetary help offered by various executive departments is contained in *The Federal Handbook for Small Business,* which has been mentioned in previous chapters.

11

WHAT PRIVATE GROUPS CAN HELP?

What about getting management help from private sources? Aside from governmental advice and assistance, what management counseling is available to you from trade and professional associations, and from other private, non-governmental agencies?

Does the management consultant, for example, have anything to offer the small businessman? What about such sources as university counseling services, certified public accountants, suppliers, lawyers, bankers, business associates—and even business competitors? Can you learn anything from them?

Bill Duff took over the operation of a small retail store in Utah. A wise initial move would have been for him to hire a certified public accountant to look over the bookkeeping system of the former owner and to explore the tax setup. Instead Bill asked a neighbor who worked in the local bank's bookkeeping section to come in two or three nights a week to do the store's accounting. "Who is better equipped to keep books than a bank employee?" he reasoned.

Bill's neighbor, however, in spite of his undoubted ability to keep faultless records, had absolutely no experience in tax matters, as a counseling team from the nearby University of Utah discovered.

The team came to Bill's store as a part of an experiment to determine the best methods of counseling small businessmen, and Bill was wise enough to accept their advice. In short order, the team discovered several glaring omissions in the accounting which put Bill in a disadvantageous tax position.

In the first place, Bill had not set up the contingent liability of the former owner as a formal debt of the business. He also had failed to recognize as debt the personal capital he had invested in the corporation. Certain activities performed by members of his family —such as having his wife mail statements and deliver merchandise—were not set up as costs to the business. When all these factors were taken into consideration, Bill's tax position changed considerably.

This is a clear-cut case of management weakness— the prime reason businesses fail, as I underscored in the last chapter. Compounding this problem is the fact that most businessmen in trouble do not take action or seek advice even when danger signals are perfectly apparent. They muddle along, somehow hoping that "things will level off" and that "tomorrow things will be better." Tomorrow, however, bankruptcy proceedings may begin.

Bill Duff was lucky. Early in the game a big weakness in his business was discovered (quite by accident!), diagnosed, and set right. True, this one factor alone might never have become serious enough to undermine Bill's whole operation, but it would have made a big difference in his profit picture. The experience was valuable to Bill in another way: it alerted him to his need for counseling. Since then he has set out in a systematic way to get advice on other facets of his business, realizing that it is no disgrace to admit that he doesn't know everything. There is no reason why you can't do the same.

In this chapter I'd like to discuss and evaluate briefly private management help available to you, some of it for the asking, some only on payment of a fee—which may, nevertheless, prove to be the most profitable investment you ever made in your business.

Where you go for assistance depends a great deal on what you think your specific problems are. A recent survey among various private management assistance agencies shows that trade associations tend to emphasize help on personnel problems, customer relations, taxes and other government-related problems, technical operating problems, costs, and advertising.

Community development organizations

Community development organizations give assistance in the same areas as do trade associations, and also aid in physical environment problems such as parking, zoning, police protection, location, and transportation.

Management counseling

Management consultants are contacted primarily for help with taxes, financing, legal problems, personnel problems, organization (that is, the legal form a business should take), competition, public relations and advertising, and problems with government. Banks and accountants give assistance in financing, bookkeeping, financial statements, taxes, and general management.

It has been estimated that there are 35,000 to 40,000 persons doing professional management counseling full time in some 1,250 to 1,700 management consultant firms in this country. These firms range in size from organizations having less than five members to large firms having several hundred.

Despite these seemingly impressive numbers, however, it is doubtful whether more than 1 per cent of small firms receives formal counseling in any one year. The small business retailer is even less likely to use available management counseling services than the small manufacturer. While it would be foolish to advise every small businessman who is in trouble to run to a management consultant firm, these figures indicate that many more could be making use of them.

Perhaps the biggest single reason small businessmen hestitate to use management consultant services is the conviction that "Those who can, do; those who can't, teach." "If the management consultant is so good," they say, "why isn't he using all his knowledge in his own business enterprise?"

This naïve attitude overlooks several important factors. First of all (as those who engage a competent management consultant will find out!), you will pay—and pay quite adequately indeed—for good advice.

Secondly, the management consultant is a member of a team. If his firm is a top-flight one, the consultant has a decided advantage over all but the most experienced and highly trained people; he has the resources of his firm to draw upon—the combined experience of specialists in research and development, marketing, production, finance and control, and personnel.

Your first consideration in choosing a management consultant should be to make certain that he is qualified to give you the help you need. Do not hesitate to discuss in great detail his qualifications. If he is qualified, he will be straightforward and matter-of-fact about giving you his complete background and references. If he hedges, drop him. A large, growing concern may be able to afford the luxury of occasional bad advice, but a small, struggling concern cannot.

Once you are certain that you have found your man, you must be willing to give him enough time and trust to enable him to do a good job for you. If you feel you cannot trust him and his firm enough to put your cards on the table, holding nothing back, this indicates that he is not the man for you.

One good criterion for judging your prospective consultant is whether he is willing to roll up his sleeves, get out in your shop or office, and really work with your staff. His function, particularly in the small business setup, is to get a working knowledge of your business, to evaluate the performance of those who have key functions, and to help train them in the areas in which they lack skill. He cannot do this without spending time with your staff. You must give him the freedom to do this without interference or restraint.

Some small business consultants work out an arrangement in which they come to your business one day a week to work with you, make suggestions, set goals for the coming week, and leave the initiative to your staff. Gradually the time the consultant spends on your premises is reduced to a day a month, and in the end he may be retained on an "on call" basis—available as new problems arise.

The advantages of this kind of arrangement are obvious; because his time is being utilized by seven or eight small companies simultaneously, the consultant will cost you far less than he would on a full-time basis. Moreover his assistance will be spread over a longer period of time and needed changes in your business can be gradual. Thus you can avoid the upheaval of sudden reorganization.

University facilities

If you are near a university with a strong business school you should investigate the possibility not only of attending business conferences and seminars, but also of engaging counseling help. A number of professors in schools of business do part-time management counseling in their specialized fields. Such services may be extended on an informal basis, even if there is no organized department in the school offering counseling.

It has been estimated that only 10 per cent of qualified professors are active in counseling, and that each of these has, on the average, only five clients per year. This means that you have an excellent chance of finding highly qualified consultants at your local university. If you are in need of help, do not dismiss the idea of seeking university counseling without investigation. Today most of those who teach in good business schools have had sound, practical business experience in addition to their theoretical training.

Moreover, the professor in a school of business has the same advantage as the member of a management consultant firm: expert, qualified associates with many different specialties. Not only does he constantly discuss contemporary business problems with them, but if need be, he can also seek additional help and counsel from them concerning your own particular business difficulties.

Local banks

Banks also play an important role in management counseling. Your banker—particularly if your business is in a small town or in a well-defined neighborhood center—probably knows more about your venture, as well as local business conditions in general, than any other single person in the area. A few banks have even established excellent formal programs to assist small business. The Bank of America, for example—a California institution with 750 branches throughout the state—has a small business advisory service through which men and women in business for themselves receive, without charge, the benefit of the bank's years of business and banking experience.

But even though your local banker may not have packaged his counseling services and given them a formal title, he can still deal very effectively with many of your business problems. He has a decided advantage over many other business counselors; you go to him when you have a real problem, so you're more likely to listen to and heed his advice.

Other private sources

The services and assistance offered by some 3,000 local chambers of commerce and other businessmen's associations and clubs are too well known to detail here. You are the best judge of whether or not membership in your local chamber, Rotary, or Kiwanis is worthwhile. It will be the exceptional case, however, in which such membership is not desirable.

In a recent survey covering a substantial number of small businesses, over 90 per cent of the proprietors indicated that they had faced at least one major difficulty in the operation of their firms within the previous two years. In the same survey a number of management service agencies were queried. Three-fifths of these agencies indicated that small businessmen are seeking their services in increasing numbers; all but 4 per cent of the remaining agencies said that the number of their small business customers is, at least, not declining.

The survey pointed up three major reasons for the increasing use of management counsel by small businessmen. First of all, business has become more complex, competition more fierce, and government regulations and requirements more demanding. Secondly, the small businessman himself is more sophisticated. Better trained and educated, he is more aware of the need for and the value of outside assistance. And finally, the agencies themselves have become more active in seeking out the small businessman and showing him the advantage of counsel.

While much help is available, there is still a definite shortage of top-flight counseling services, public and private, in many communities. Congress is taking an interest in this problem, and studies are now under way to see if more effective ways can be found to make competent counseling available to you when you need it.

Even the services that are available, however, are not used as much as they might be by small business. A vast number of small businessmen, either out of pride or ignorance, refuse to take advantage of them. Three attitudes seem to characterize small businessmen with respect to counseling. First there is the wide-awake, ambitious, and open-minded attitude that characterizes those who seek counseling either before going into business or when a problem crops up after the business is under way. Secondly, there is the passive attitude of those who are willing to listen to and sometimes use advice if it is spoon-fed to them and if it doesn't cost them any effort. Finally there is the "don't bother me" attitude, characterizing the businessmen who refuse to ask or accept advice from anyone at any time. These are the ones who fade silently—by the thousands—out of the business picture.

Good advice properly applied can be of tremendous help to you. The operation of a business today, small or large, has become highly complicated. You show shrewdness when you recognize that you, as a businessman, need advice at various times. You show commendable common sense when you are able to make good use of such advice in time of business crisis, or better still, when you are able to use it to solve your problems well before a panic period sets in.

12

TRADE ASSOCIATIONS: HELP
OR HURT?

Can good advice, judgment, and care solve your problems before you start? Some of them, yes. All of them, never. Every practical situation is different. How will you know what all of your problems will be until you actually face them? You won't.

Chances are, however, that others in your business have run into problems that you yourself may face. Your trade association, then, may be able to help you in a number of ways. You may want to join it.

In 1956 the Chamber of Commerce of the United States defined trade associations as follows:

> A typical trade association is a voluntary non-profit organization that draws its members—firms and individuals —usually from a specific field of business and undertakes activities especially designed to assist its members to improve the branch of commerce they represent and, ultimately, to serve the public.

There are few nationally known trade associations that derive their membership solely from small businessmen. Most associations draw their members from a "specific field of business." Small business members like yourself, however, make up the largest group of individuals who belong to most trade associations.

There are, in effect, two types of association organization. First there is the "federated" type, in which you must first join a state, and/or regional association before joining the national association. In the second, "direct member" type, you are not required to join local or state groups prior to affiliation with the national organization.

You will discover that the most important services rendered to association members are management assistance programs. Some of these aids are very complete and elaborate; others are relatively simple. One of the latest is a management training manual prepared by the American Motor Hotel Association.

This manual deals with such important aspects of proper motel operation as land planning and economic feasibility, taxes, accounting and financing controls, legal problems, financing, purchasing, design, construction and interior decoration, personnel, sales promotion and merchandising, group business and catering, motel management and operation, and restaurant operation.

The Restaurant Association of Metropolitan Washington also offers a personnel referral service to its members. This service does not take the place of employment agencies, but it does aid the members of the association in locating qualified and experienced personnel.

Through bulletins, meetings, and personal calls from association executives, you also will be kept informed about various improved management methods in marketing, personnel, finance, and production.

Associations also conduct public relation programs designed to bring to the attention of the public the role of the particular industry. Your association will suggest advertising campaigns for you to use in your home town. It may also engage in national advertising, from which you also will derive benefit.

Another important function of an association is to provide an effective governmental relations program for its industry. Most trade associations have Washington offices, staffed by experts who attempt to make the best possible impression on members of Congress and congressional staffs. The efforts of such offices are directed toward keeping Congress informed as to the part your industry plays in the over-all economic life of the country. To use the Madison Avenue term, it tries to present the "image" of your industry in the best possible light.

The association keeps you informed on pending legislative matters and regulation changes in governmental administrative agencies. It also asks the views of the various members on a particular subject in order to formulate an industry position, and organizes programs to present these views on legislative matters. Associations acquaint legislators with many details of their industries that would otherwise be unavailable. An association can do this because of its more intimate knowledge of the industry. Association representatives also present testimony to legislative committees and appear before governmental regulatory commissions and agencies.

Many national association executives are experts on legislative procedures, and are able to present the position of their industries clearly and concisely. This is a very valuable service to busy legislators.

The best representatives also are able to answer questions with the precision that comes only with a complete understanding of the subject. They are able to indicate with what authority they speak for the group they represent. Members of Congress are very skeptical of the man who claims to represent the views of tens of thousands of association members on particular legislation, but can point to no convention, referendum, or even executive board action to support his position. They also tend to discount trade association executives who are clumsy and inept in their presentation of their association's positions regarding legislation.

Most associations have developed codes of ethics and trade practice rules for their members. The penalty, however, for breach of these ethics and rules is in no way comparable to the breach of a professional code of ethics by a doctor or a lawyer. Public opinion demands strict adherence to these and other professional codes. Trade associations are generally not able to punish breaches in their established codes, and until professional standards are established for business I doubt whether they ever will be able to do this.

Trade standards can, however, help protect you from the shady operations of some industry members. These standards also are important in the industry's public relations program, and may be a great morale-booster, helping build up a pride which results in a stronger industry.

Many associations have taken the lead in research programs designed to improve the products or services of their industries. These programs have helped to increase the sale of members' products, and have led to the development of valuable new sales promotion ideas.

In spite of their excellent services, many improvements could be made in these associations. Even though associations are made up primarily of small businesses, often they do not serve the real needs of their smaller members. This is partly their fault and partly the fault of the small businessman.

The small businessman is by nature an individualist. He wants to be his own boss and run things his own way. He does not like someone trying to help him even if he knows he needs advice, and he has very little time or desire to read the many business pamphlets and other aids that are made available by his association. He has neither the time nor the money to indulge himself in the luxury of a trade association convention in Miami or Atlantic City. Therefore, he usually does not make good use of the programs offered by his association.

The trade association often presents its programs in such a manner that they are of little use to the small businessman. Highly technical programs on taxation, marketing, accounting, and so on may be fine for those businesses which employ specialists in these various departments, but they are too advanced for the one-man operation. Management aids in accounting problems prepared for CPAs would have little meaning to smaller association members, who have very simple accounting systems. And, ironically, it is the owner-operated business that most needs the aids offered by the trade association.

The associations, then, should attempt to design their programs in all aspects of the trade—sales marketing, finance, and advertising—to reach their members in the most effective way. They should try as hard as possible to reach those smaller small businesses with management aids that can be quickly understood. Most small businessmen have very little leisure, and the use of attractively presented illuminated slides or cartoons, for example, could provide an excellent, easily understood program for a man too busy to read an involved technical pamphlet.

Aids should be aimed at the immediate management problems of the small members if they are to be of real value. There is very little practical help to be gained by a small businessman in a program on long-range planning if his immediate problem is staying in business from week to week. A well thought-out, adequately presented program devoted to the establishment of branches will not interest the man who is trying to keep the doors to his one store open.

There is also a question of whether an association can render the best service on a local or national basis. There are, of course, advantages in both emphases. The local agency can better meet problems that arise on the local level; the national agency can get a better over-all picture of the entire industry. The national organization also has had a great wealth of experience in handling questions of its members all over the country, questions which may be similar to your own. So often the individual member does not realize and appreciate the very real work that the national organization does. The national organization may not only be of direct help to the member, but will help indirectly through its work with state and local associations. As more and more of our interests are being centered in Washington, the strength and influence of the national associations have increased.

It is very likely, however, that you will respond more readily and benefit more from assistance from your state or local association. Officials of your local association are more likely to pay personal visits to your business. There is a greater chance that real friendship and trust will develop between you and the association's state and local executives, rather than between you and the national executives. Although you may learn to appreciate the efforts of the national organization, day-to-day help will be furnished by state and local officials.

There is much unused help available to you from your trade association, and you should make every effort to get your money's worth out of your membership. If you have a problem, ask the association representative about it when he visits you. If you are not visited regularly, write to national headquarters for the latest information on your problem. If association headquarters doesn't have it, demand that adequate information and advice be obtained for you.

There is much more the association can do to make its programs more responsive to your needs. Mutual cooperation and understanding will result in greater benefit to you, your association, and to the country.

Will The Big Boys Crush You?

13

SHOULD YOU SELL OUT OR MERGE?

What can a small businessman do, faced with competition from a large chain? Or a small manufacturer, denied the right to purchase by a supplier with a strangle-hold on certain key materials like aluminum, copper, and cement? Or a retailer, forced to tie in unwanted products to retain his dealership?

Of course, he can sell out. Or go into bankruptcy. Or "sue and be damned," as a big oil company salesman told one of his company's independent gasoline station operators.

But all of these prospects are grim. Is there no other way out? Threatened with being engulfed by big business, can you stay in the ring and compete?

The American dairy products industry has been called "clearly the most merger-prone." In the United States, eight large firms sell more than half the frozen milk products to retail outlets, and control nearly as much of the fluid milk trade. Between 1923 and 1961, these eight giants acquired 2,000 small companies.

The big dairy chains typically move into a new territory and lure accounts away from local ice cream manufacturers and dairies with unmatchable (for the little fellow) offers of free ice cream storage and freezer cabinets. Often too, they use the attraction of big discounts and rebates.

The Cloverleaf Dairy, a small concern in a midwestern community, decided to package milk in gallon containers and retail it at a price three cents below the retail cost of four one-quart containers. It took two branches of large national concerns just three months to put Cloverleaf out of business, for they were able to sell milk in all sizes of containers far below normal retail cost in Cloverleaf territory, making it up in other areas. Needless to say their prices went up soon after Cloverleaf announced bankruptcy.

In this case, the big companies did not even have the incentive to buy Cloverleaf out. They knew that Cloverleaf's fresh milk suppliers would have no alternative but to sell to them once Cloverleaf was out of the way, and that any remaining Cloverleaf customers would, of course, have no alternative retailers from whom to buy.

James Dooley, a small California merchant, was threatened by Big A, a chain of variety stores. Big A published an eight-page ad, each page listing a fantastic come-on: nylons at nine cents a pair, ironing board covers for thirty-eight cents, a pound of coffee as a free gift to each household, and so on.

Unable to match such largesse, Dooley sued under a California statute which prohibits selling below cost if the intent is to injure competition. Dooley also was able to get (again under California law) a temporary injunction ordering Big A to cease selling below cost while the case was being tried. Thus Dooley was at least able to insure that, if he won his case, he would still be in business to enjoy the victory.

Few small businessmen in other parts of the country would have any such recourse. Under present Federal Trade Commission regulations, preliminary injunctions are impossible. The FTC can issue only permanent orders to "cease and desist"—*after* the case is won. But this may take years and the patient may die in the meantime, even though the operation eventually succeeds.

Empire Products, a small Pacific Coast steel fabricator, faces another type of monopoly. In effect, only two steel companies serve the area, and because of the "basing-point" system it is impractical for big eastern companies to sell steel in this location in times of shortage, since they do not serve it when steel is in abundant supply.

This means that two giants exercise absolute control over the fate of small fabricators like Empire. In times of abundance, Empire will get the steel it needs, but in times of shortage steel will be allocated in a ratio set by the big suppliers and determined by the volume Empire customarily buys. In times of severe shortage, then, Empire may very well get no steel at all, since many big steel companies themselves have now expanded vertically into fabricating. In this case, big steel's own fabricating facilities are certain to be supplied first. Companies like Empire, faced with long periods of critical shortage, may have no alternative but to sell out.

All these cases transgress an ancient right, deeply rooted in Anglo–Saxon market law—the consumer's right to buy. Essentially, this means that anyone setting himself up in the market place as a business, as opposed to occasional transactions between private citizens, must extend certain "market rights" to anyone coming to the market place. In a true free enterprise system, commodities must go to the highest bidders on a strictly impersonal basis. In a monopolistic system, such a free flow of goods between seller and buyer becomes almost impossible. The extra profits to be reaped by the seller are too enticing, and refusal to sell becomes a tool to effect an ever-increasing concentration of power in the hands of the seller.

The rivals of Cloverleaf exercised a vicious sort of price discrimination by selling the same class of goods, with no additional features or services, at a lower price in one market in order to put a competitor out of business. Big A illegally restricted the right to buy in limiting its specials "one to a customer"—a dead giveaway that the goods were intended only to injure competition and were not a free offer of goods to all comers. In a free market, the whole quantity of special goods would have had to be sold to any one customer who desired to buy it. Empire was also clearly discriminated against. In a free market, the seller must offer his wares to all, without discrimination.

As I will discuss in Chapter 15, present-day anti-trust laws simply are inadequate to deal with these and similar problems of the small businessman. Until Congress can strengthen these laws there will not be any way out for many a little fellow, once big business gives him a hungry look.

The first movement toward business mergers at the turn of the century created many of the industrial giants which have endured to this day: the American Tobacco Company, the U. S. Rubber Company, and U. S. Steel. During the second merger wave in the 1920's, many of the industrial leaders increased their holdings and also dipped down into some of the characteristically small business industries to effect "vertical integration." The auto industry, for example, began manufacturing more and more of its own parts and components.

In the late 1920's, too, the supermarket was born, and small store units began to give way to the chains. The tactics of the chain stores are used even today: lowering prices in one region to win small store customers while making up the loss in another, forcing wholesalers to give discounts to chain store accounts while denying them to independents, and so on.

The "war against the chains" was a topic of conversation in every household and in the news and business periodicals of the time. "Outlaw the Chain Store Menace," "Support the Anti-Chain Store League," and "Recapture Freedom of Opportunity" were typical headlines of the day.

Alarmed at the chain trend, Congress at one point considered passing a law to "freeze" the number of chains. There was also an attempt to create what pro-chain apologists called a "punitive" tax on every store added to a chain above a certain number. Some states actually did pass tax measures designed to discourage additions to chains; New Jersey, for example, imposed a $10,000 license fee on supermarkets.

The chain stores fought back vigorously, charging that such legislation against them represented "laws against the consumer's pocketbook" and "punishing efficiency." A & P, after many years of silence, took full page ads to present the case for chain stores. "Why tax the poor man's store?" lamented Chain Store Age in a typical article in 1935.

The Depression hurt the chains. By 1937, A & P had closed 1,200 stores and its profits had dropped 46 per cent. During World War II, the chain stores barely held their own. In the past decade, however, the movement toward ever-increasing concentration has begun anew, and today it has reached alarming heights. In 1929, for example, only 4 per cent of all food stores sold over $300,000 worth of merchandise. Today, 70 per cent of all food stores sell that amount. The chains have succeeded in gobbling up, in the ten-year period between 1949 and 1958, 2,490 independent food stores!

Two-thirds of these—1,660—were purchased by the ten largest chains.

The big chain food stores, in addition to moving out horizontally to take over some 85 per cent of the total grocery trade (this includes corporate food chain retailers and groups of affiliated retailers), have also set the pace for the so-called vertical integration movement. A typical chain may, besides owning its wholesale house, operate thirty or forty bakeries, canneries, cheese plants, creameries, and coffee roasting plants. Indeed, a chain food concern may derive as much as 30 to 40 per cent of its profits from its manufacturing subsidiaries.

It is evident that there has been a steady increase in business concentration in general in the years since World War II. Nor has this merger movement shown any signs as yet of losing its momentum.

In the decade between 1951 and 1961, 3,404 smaller firms were acquired by the 500 largest companies in the United States. Acquisitions were highest in dairy products, paper and chemicals, aerospace components, refining, electrical equipment, motor vehicles, and textiles. It is interesting to note that the merger movement, while still going on in the areas typical of big business activity—metals, rubber, glass—has also affected to a greater extent than ever before two fields which have traditionally been strongholds of the small businessman; textiles and apparel, and food and dairy products.

All this means that as a small businessman you have a tough problem—and one on a national scale. Yet in spite of the difficulties, I believe that the small businessman with determination and ingenuity still can succeed, particularly in those lines of business where bigness does not necessarily mean efficiency. Indeed, in many lines of retailing, in a large number of service industries, and in certain lines of manufacturing, such as the production of automotive and electronics components, it is the opinion of experts that the small firm is actually more efficient.

You will have some help from Uncle Sam—through the Federal Trade Commission and the Department of Justice—in your fight to stay afloat. Frankly, however, this assistance will be meager. I will go into the subject in greater detail in Chapter 15. Also, friends of small business in Congress have waged a long battle to strengthen the antitrust laws and the executive agencies which administer them; I'll have more to say about this aspect of the merger and monopoly problem in Chapter 21.

14

CAN YOU BREAK INTO A SHOPPING CENTER?

"After the land across the street was cleared for the new shopping center, the first sign to go up was a big one announcing that a large chain drug company would soon build a store over there.

"I see this sign every morning as I go to open up. It reminds me that my days are numbered."

So testified Samuel Morris, a partner in the Hillandale Pharmacy, a bright, neat, retail drugstore on busy New Hampshire Avenue in suburban Silver Spring, Maryland. In 1959, Sam came to tell his story at a special Senate hearing on practices excluding small business concerns from suburban shopping centers. Sam spoke not only for himself but for seven other small businessmen, who run a dry cleaning establishment, a flower and gift shop, a local chain dairy store, a pizza restaurant, a barbershop, a hardware store, and a radio and TV shop on his strip on New Hampshire Avenue.

Recently I drove to Silver Spring and stood on Sam's corner. The Hillandale Shopping Center is a reality now—shiny, new, and attractive—right across the highway from Sam. And this young proprietor, a seasoned and highly successful local businessman, is still on the outside looking in. So are six of the other seven. Only the hardware store made the grade. As small businessmen they weren't able either to lick 'em *or* join 'em.

Right after the war, Sam Morris started with a small drugstore in Washington, near the Senate. In five years he had built up a good, flourishing business; he had proved that he "could operate a good retail drugstore successfully and profitably and pay my bills."

But the suburbs beckoned, and Sam decided he wanted to move to a young community with more growth potential. He set his heart on Silver Spring, a typical suburban area. In 1951 he took the store on New Hampshire Avenue. By 1956 he had expanded his sales volume enough to take on a partner, rent the store-front adjoining his store, buy new fixtures, and remodel his whole operation.

The people passing Sam's corner speak highly of him. The Hillandale Pharmacy has given the area real service. It prices goods competitively and has grown with the community. Sam is a friend of most of the residents. He's a charter member of the county pharmaceutical society, the local citizens' association, and the local businessmen's group. He serves on community boards and committees.

Sam is not outside the shopping center because he didn't try to get in.

"In 1956," he says, "after we'd expanded the store to better serve the needs of the community, we learned that this large plot of land across from us had been optioned to build a shopping center. One of our customers turned out to be the prime developer. When he was in the store one day, we approached him about the drugstore space in the new center. He tried to discourage us, saying he felt it would not be possible to lease to us.

"We pressed him for reasons why we couldn't be considered, as we were known in the community and had proven our ability to keep up with the community's needs, almost doubling our floor space in a little over five years' time.

"He told us it was due to loan matters—money problems. I found out later that he meant he couldn't take us in because shopping center developers have to get most of their leases from concerns with AAA–1 credit ratings in order to get long-term loans to build. This means chains—no local man has that kind of rating.

"Then the financiers pass the buck by saying that their hands too, are tied. They have to invest their stockholders' money in safe ventures.

"So in the end, there isn't anyone you can actually put your finger on to blame for the situation. But the fact is, we're being hurt today and hurt badly. At the moment we're relying on our prescription business. According to the experts, however, no druggist can exist for long on prescriptions alone. So we're looking for a new location."

Sam Morris is not afraid of competition. He's sure that he could outmerchandise and outsell the chain store if he could meet it on an equal footing. But the odds are against Sam Morris and his associates. He and the six other small merchants have customer parking space for only twenty-four cars, while the shopping center parks 2,000.

"New Hampshire is a busy, main thoroughfare," Sam says. "We can't afford to build a pedestrian underpass, and you can bet your life the developers of that shopping center won't do it for us. We just aren't able to attract customers across the street from the available parking space—even if we'd be willing to sell our goods at a loss. It's just too far to walk.

"And since we can't expand our parking facilities, the shopping center is slowly drying us up as going businesses."

The case of Sam Morris is typical of that of many small merchants across the country who are unable to lease space in shopping centers. Shopping centers come in all sizes: neighborhood, community, regional. The little fellow has trouble getting into any of them, even if he is willing to pay more rent than the chains.

The strange thing is that a developer may prefer a local merchant to a chain. He must, however, produce prime leases—concerns with AAA–1 credit ratings—in order to get long-term financing. Unfortunately local chains, even of five to ten supermarkets or variety stores, don't have this kind of rating. Indeed, the developer often has to let space go to a chain for less than it is really worth in order to entice the chain to come in.

And the chain often proves to be the developer's "loss leader."

Thus hundreds of small, able merchants, men who have pioneered in their own communities and made good, are shut out of the new, modern facilities they want, need, and can pay for.

And, as mentioned above, it's far from "business as usual" at the old locations. From the day these shopping centers open, they dramatically drain off business from the traditional neighborhood and downtown shopping areas, planned and built before the automobile age. For there's no place to park in these downtown areas; parking may be located blocks away from the stores. So the shopping center opens. And from that day, the small merchant finds himself on the back streets of trade. Today there are approximately 6,000 shopping centers actually operating. Some 10,000 are expected to be doing business by the end of 1965.

Now that we've looked at the shopping center from Sam Morris' point of view, let's look at the problem from where George Jensen sits. George is a developer —and now the renting agent—for a community-size shopping center of thirty stores. Five years ago he took his idea for it to his attorney, and the two men formed a syndicate with the prospective architect and builder.

George's first move was to engage a good market analyst. He had to be sure his site was just the right one: it couldn't be too close to another shopping center

—or to a site which might some day be used for one. There were endless meetings to pore over data on prospective customers in the trading area: store sales, number of charge accounts, bank deposits and savings accounts, level of incomes. Then the group looked over patterns of auto traffic, capacities of highways adjacent to the site. And they didn't fail to investigate long-range city and highway planning.

Finally, what George hoped was just the right site was chosen, and the deal for the land closed. George and his associates were lucky, and were able to do this by bringing the landowner into their syndicate. Like many developers, they had little ready cash, and at this point were contributing their services without compensation.

The next step, as you might expect, was to find the cool $2 million they needed to finance the construction and to provide operating capital for the first few months, until tenants got settled and rents began coming in. Local banks were willing to provide short-term capital to start building, but only if long-term financing was in sight.

Now George Jensen couldn't simply walk into a big insurance company, spread his plans out on the table, and expect to get long-term financing. The only way he could get the money he needed was to *sign up his key tenants first.* Before even one brick was laid upon another he had to go out and get firm commitments from his major stores—which he calls his "bell-cow tenants" because they ring in the biggest volume of customers.

This is the crucial point at which the Sam Morrises—in hundreds of cases documented throughout the land —are told they can't get in.

What is to be done for local merchants like Sam Morris and his friends? Even as you read this, they are being slowly squeezed out. Sam is looking for a new store. He is going to try again, but he is discouraged.

"Will we start again," he asks, "building a small store into a bigger one—pioneering—and then, when the community gets large enough and the retail drug business volume big enough, will someone build another shopping center across the street from us and lease the new building to a chain?

"I have some new ideas on what we could do with layout and traffic and lighting in a new, modern, 6,000 or 7,000-foot store with ample parking space around it. Will we ever get a chance to risk our money and time and ingenuity to try it out?"

The answer is no, I'm afraid. The answer will continue to be no until we break the monopolistic stranglehold that chains have on store locations in shopping centers. To do this we must strengthen and broaden our antitrust laws, as I will discuss in the next chapter.

Moreover, we need specific legislation to put the independent merchant on an equal footing with the chain in the shopping center situation. One solution might be to provide lease insurance for the small businessman who wants to get into a shopping center. A bill to insure such leases has been introduced in the present session of Congress. If it passes it will provide the small businessman with a substitute for a national credit rating and protect the shopping center developers, many of whom would like to take in local merchants. This and other actions that Congress can take are discussed in Chapter 21.

15

OUR ANTIMONOPOLY LAWS: ARE
THEY GOOD ENOUGH?

You may never have had to deal firsthand with the threat of monopoly—"the curse of bigness," as Justice Brandeis once termed it. Unlike Cloverleaf Dairy or Empire Products, the small firms described in Chapter 13, you may never have personally been forced out of your business by a big chain food or variety store. But you have been deeply affected, as small businessman, as a consumer, and simply as a citizen, by the growing concentration of business and manufacturing in every sector of the American economy.

Make no mistake about it! Our antitrust laws and their enforcement are crucial; we are dealing here with nothing less than a question of power in our society. And not just economic power. For political and economic power are intermeshed in American life.

Of course, no one would be so foolish as to advocate doing away with many of our large firms, which function so efficiently simply because they *are* large enough to be able to use mass-production techniques effectively.

A Ford plant, for example, employing thousands of workers and turning out hundreds of autos a day, is an American marvel. It is also Big Business, with capital letters. Big business that is thoroughly justified.

But even the auto plant has its effective size limitation. And it has yet to be proved that competition is fostered by one auto manufacturer hungrily gulping down the plants of its rivals and, moreover, merging vertically. Most automobile manufacturers today control every operation, from mining, transporting the ore, and manufacturing the smallest components, to retailing, via the supposedly independent home town dealer.

There are certain myths that the big fellows use in trying to allay our fears that they are taking over.

What I like to call the "numbers" myth is the most persistent. Big businessmen will tell you that, statistically, the total number of small businesses has never dropped below 92 per cent of all firms. How then can we fear the spectre of monopoly when big fellows control a mere 8 or 10 per cent of the business firms?

Two, however, can play this numbers game. Statistically, it can be proved that concentration in all business and manufacturing has been increasing steadily since the turn of the century.

By 1905, 10 per cent of U. S. firms controlled *40 per cent of all manufacturing capital* in the country. Today, that "modest" 10 per cent of *all business*—the big firms —controls between 65 and 70 per cent of the total output of all businesses!

Closely related to the numbers myth is the claim that the big fellows actually have fostered hundreds of new small businesses by subcontracting work on small parts (in the auto and airplane industries particularly) to little firms. A popular magazine not long ago carried the soul-rending article, "How Big Business Hatches Little Business." I thought the title could very well be altered to reflect the real situation in subcontracting by changing the word "hatches" to "hatchets." Anyone familiar with the weird world of subcontracting knows that the small independent plant, more often than not, becomes nothing more than an appendage of the prime contractor, with all managerial functions assumed by the latter on a take-it-or-leave-it basis.

Big chain entrepreneurs also like to use the "we control only" myth. The chain grocers are particularly fond of this argument. With a perfectly straight face they will tell you that the A & P, after all, "controls only" 12 per cent of the grocery business across the country. They carefully forget to mention that the large chains, which typically grow out in concentric circles, may do *up to 40 or 50 per cent and even more* of all the food business in their areas, as Safeway does in Texas and New Mexico.

Another argument the big fellows advance in the sweet name of efficiency and lower prices is the completely fallacious claim that mergers do not necessarily do away with competition; in fact, they say, mergers may *increase* it. One giant dominating a field can, of course, pretty well dictate to whom it will sell and at what price. But, the argument runs, if a medium-sized firm can, through merger, also become a giant, and there are two, three, or even four giants already in the field, the giants can at least clobber each other—all to the ultimate benefit of the consumer.

I think the one recent example of the scandalous price-fixing by two giants, Westinghouse and General Electric, shows the weakness of this argument. The temptation to reap the fantastic profits that are possible because of absolute control of a market is too great when just a few key men in a few companies can get together to fix prices.

If an industry were divided among, say, 100 smaller electric appliance manufacturers, nothing much would be lost in the way of efficiency. Each manufacturer would still be large enough to utilize the most modern plant methods and techniques. And collusion to fix prices would be pretty difficult among 100 competitors. Someone would simply refuse to collaborate—or would squeal. As one writer astutely points out, the effects of oligopoly, the domination of an industry by a few giants, are pretty hard to discern from pure monopoly.

Thurmand Arnold, former assistant attorney general in charge of the Antitrust Division of the Justice Department, summed up the situation in these words:

Fundamentally, the great organizations are cannibalistic. . . . United States Steel . . . swallows up many smaller organizations by doing things which the smaller organizations could do just as well. There is no reason in the world why United States Steel should do what can be done in Pueblo, Colorado, by smaller organizations—for example, making nails.

It is the elimination of smaller businessmen and capital in smaller communities through integration that is the great evil. . . . Integration, once accomplished, cannot be undone; it is awfully hard to ever put the independent businessman back. . . .

What is the United States government doing about this "curse of bigness" that threatens the small businessman on every side? Not very much. But it will be most valuable to outline that little bit for you.

To be blunt, the safeguards designed to protect you as a small businessman—as flimsy as they were to begin with—are being pretty steadily eroded away. Judicial limitations have eaten into them. They have been further vitiated by the current government practice of settling many antitrust cases out of court by consent decree, thus preventing the small businessman from using any government evidence for his own, related private damage suit. Moreover, even though the fines for violations have been increased, the amounts exacted are still small in relation to the monopolist's potential profit. It is still worth his while to go ahead with some predatory business practice, for he may very well get away with it. If he doesn't, the penalties will be comparatively negligible anyway. I shall return to these specific difficulties later on in this chapter.

To understand just how the antitrust laws work—

and your stake in them as a small businessman—it's necessary to look for a moment at the Sherman Act and the Clayton Act, both designed to guard trade and commerce from overconcentration of economic power in any business or industry and to outlaw business practices judged to promote monopoly. These two acts were later reinforced by the Robinson–Patman Act, aimed at injurious pricing practices.

All these laws are administered and enforced by the Department of Justice and the Federal Trade Commission, although the emphasis is different in each agency.

The Federal Trade Commission was designed to render you, as a businessman and a consumer, much more direct aid than the Justice Department. The FTC administers a wide variety of laws, from those preventing unfair or deceptive methods of competition to those preventing false advertising and price discrimination. It also investigates and reports to the Attorney General violations of antitrust laws by corporations. In a word, the philosophy governing the FTC is that all competitors—large and small—should begin the race from the same starting point.

Any person, corporation, or organization may ask the FTC to investigate what he believes to be a violation of the laws under its jurisdiction. Since the commission acts only in the public interest, you will not be considered a party to any action, nor will your name be divulged in the usual course of FTC proceedings.

To make a complaint, simply write (no special forms

are needed) what you believe to be the particular violations of the Federal Trade Commission Act, sign your name, and mail it to the FTC, Washington, D. C. The FTC will give you an "advisory opinion" on whether some business practice or proposed course of action would violate FTC law.

A big handicap of the FTC is its lack of real power to enforce its decisions. It is a policeman empowered to guard the laws, but given the right only to say "No! Stop!" It has no club or weapon to make a violator cease and desist if he refuses to do so.

The Justice Department, with its Antitrust Division and antitrust activities, is not specifically designed as a service agency for the small businessman. It does, however, have the power to prosecute antitrust violations and to inflict penalties. In theory, therefore, in maintaining competition as the keynote of the American economy, the Justice Department should (indirectly, it is true) foster the growth and prosperity of small business.

Antitrust laws are extremely complex, however. To get a decision—and make it stick on appeal—is a long and tortuous process; the litigation sometimes goes on for twenty-five to thirty years. The department is also restricted by funds and personnel in the number of cases it can handle, requiring it to choose carefully which giants it will take on.

It was the intent of Congress that the antitrust laws and the regulatory agencies set up to administer them would do two things. First, they would initiate actions to discourage monopoly and improve the over-all climate for competition. The benefits of such actions for the small businessman would be indirect, but nonetheless real.

Secondly, the antitrust laws would give businessmen the right to file private suits directly, without waiting for government action. Not only would this give the injured man relief—indeed, the laws provide for the ancient redress of triple damages—but a small army of private plaintiffs would supplement the government's small antitrust "police force."

Just how have these two intentions of Congress worked out in practice? To be sure, in its antitrust actions the Justice Department has won some notable victories against the big trusts, improving the competitive situation for everyone. But viewed against the extent of the problem, the department's batting average tends to shrink. At least it does not offer much comfort to the small businessman facing specific problems in Oshkosh or Beaver Dam, and hoping that the often unpredictable and indirect actions of the Justice Department or the FTC will, some day, somehow, filter down to ease the particular squeeze in which he finds himself.

The Department of Justice's actions have been colored, too, by the myth I mentioned earlier: that competition is still served by two or three giants in a given industry who, nevertheless, remain truly competitive with each other. Thus much Justice Department effort goes into controlling giants in their relations *with each other,* rather than compelling them actually to divest themselves of some of their vertical acquisitions. Such a divestiture might, in the current philosophy of the department, actually injure competition by permitting one giant to become dominant.

Moreover, even in those cases in which the department has won what have seemed like notable victories (as, for example, in cases against Safeway, United Fruit, and the National Cash Register Company), the light fines and suspended sentences have provided little deterrence. Only two men have ever gone to jail in the whole history of antitrust law in the United States. The light penalties and the lack of subsequent enforcement have encouraged violators to go on doing pretty much what they were doing before.

What about the second intention of Congress in framing the antitrust laws—to give the small businessman the right to file private suit under these laws?

In the first half-century of the existence of the Sherman Act (1890 to 1940), only thirteen businessmen won their cases against the big fellows! There have been many more suits since that time, but the small businessman has won mighty few of them. Moreover, private suits under the Robinson–Patman Act have been successful in only *five* instances.

Why is this so? For one reason, as mentioned earlier, the Justice Department has tended to settle many cases out of court by consent decrees, reaching the high water mark of 83 per cent in 1957. What does this mean for the small businessman? It means that the evidence in all these cases, gathered by the government, with its unparalleled power and resources, is simply unavailable to him, no matter how pertinent it be to his own case. If he wants to pursue a suit on his own, he has to start from scratch, using his own money to gather the evidence he needs.

As pointed out by Mr. Lee Loevinger, former chief of the antitrust division of the Justice Department, now FCC commissioner, there are many obstacles facing the small businessman with a grievance against a big operator.

> As a practical matter, a small victim of antitrust violation cannot undertake any action for vindication of his rights unless he is willing and able to wait at least two or three years (and often longer) for the decision of his case, is able to advance at least several thousand dollars in probable costs of preparing and presenting his case, and is prepared to withstand the social and economic pressures and the threat of reprisal and retaliation that not infrequently are the lot of the antitrust plaintiff.

Thurmand Arnold, now an antitrust attorney in private practice, puts it even more bluntly. If anyone comes to him wanting to sue a great corporation under the antitrust laws, he says to them, "Just forget about attorneys' fees for the moment. Have you got $25,000 to put on the line immediately for expenses of depositions and things of that sort?"

The remedies? Our antitrust laws must be amended

and strengthened to carry out more faithfully the original intent of Congress in framing them. This is far from an easy prospect, because it involves powerful vested interests, on the one hand, and the slow-moving, ponderous machinery of bureaucracy on the other.

To suggest that even simple remedial measures will be easy to legislate would be to mislead you. Even so, the friends of small business in Congress will go on fighting on all possible fronts to improve the competitive climate in which you, the small businessman, can grow and flourish—and to give you the weapons to fight against being swallowed up in the tide of big business concentration.

16

WHY NOT FAIR TRADE?

Preston Wilson sells a nationally branded bicycle in his small shop in Teaneck, New Jersey. He has sold these bicycles there for the past thirty-seven years.

Wilson's business good will has been built not only on a fine product, however, but on his very complete parts and repair service. He has put much effort into this important sideline, servicing not only his own products but other brands of bicycles as well.

During his years in business, Wilson has seen many bicycle dealers come and go in his area. Bicycle retailing is extremely competitive. To make a go of it demands a lot of ingenuity and drive, and the willingness to work hard at building up extras, like an efficient repair service and a good variety of spare parts.

Now a new competitor, the discount house, is threatening Preston Wilson—and many small retailers like him throughout the land. This competitor can't be bested by more efficient service, convenience, or personal service.

In Wilson's own area, chains and discount houses

have become the dominant sellers of bicycles—and most other lines of merchandise. Indeed, a single retail outlet of a chain in Teaneck now sells as many bicycles of its own private brand as all the small bicycle dealers sell of other bicycles all over the county.

In the face of this overwhelming competition, small independents like Wilson are in deep trouble. "I cannot promote the sale of my line of bicycles and effectively compete with these large chain outlets if at the same time I must face price-cutting on the identical line I handle," Wilson says. "If those selling the same nationally branded bicycles that I sell engage in cutthroat competition among themselves, there is nothing left in it for me—or for them—to handle such products. Eventually, none of us will be left to compete with the stores handling other brands. In that case, the big get bigger and the small get smaller and fewer."

What is the answer for men like Preston Wilson? He cannot meet the chains on their own terms because he does not have the capital. Nor can he live on the crumbs, being content with his parts and repair business and servicing the bicycles sold by the big fellows whose operations are, of course, highly profitable precisely *because* they offer no extras like parts, repairs, delivery, and so on. Somehow, however, Preston Wilson's right to compete must be protected.

Wilson is confident of his own ability to compete successfully, even with the big chain stores selling other brands of bicycles, if he does not first have to engage in a price war with retailers handling his own brand.

Wilson is confident because he and his fellow dealers sell a product that is nationally known, that has proven its quality, and that has a wide public acceptance built up by the manufacturer over many years, enhanced considerably by the personal services which the independent dealers offer. The manufacturer and most of his dealers have worked hard to secure this public confidence, and they quite rightly want to protect their tremendous investment of money, time, and effort. If, however, one maverick volume dealer can offer these bicycles at a price considerably lower than the others, then the ability—and incentive—to stay in business and compete with the many other brands of bicycles disappears.

In the end, everyone loses; the retailer goes out of business, the manufacturer loses his retail outlets and often has to sacrifice quality in order to manufacture lower priced merchandise for sale in the chain discount houses, and the consumer suffers in terms of quality and price, because of the reduced competition, and the convenience and service he no longer receives from his neighborhood dealers.

It is for these reasons that the "fair trade" or "quality stabilization" bills introduced in the last several Congresses are so crucial to small business. No measure introduced in Congress in the past twenty years would do more to benefit small business and the consumer than the "Quality Stabilization Bill."

What does this bill propose? To allow the proprietor of a trademark or trade name to control the minimum retail price at which the retailer sells his branded merchandise. The law would apply, however, *only* if merchandise is in free and open competition in interstate commerce, and only if there are many other sellers of similar goods. Thus the law would enhance competition by enabling more retail dealers to stay in the ring.

This is the crux of the quality stabilization proposal. There could not be the kind of price-fixing used by lawyers and doctors to fix fees for an entire community, by big steel manufacturers to fix their prices for the whole nation, and by the federal government to fix national farm prices or minimum wages. The law would only let a manufacturer establish a retail price *if* his brand was in competition with other brands. Competition is the essential ingredient.

The law would be in no way coercive; owners of a brand could choose not to avail themselves of the authority to set minimum prices if they do not wish to do so.

"Fair trade" is not a new concept. Most states have had fair trade laws on their books for a number of years; the reason the issue has become crucial now is that these state laws are proving inadequate in the face of the tremendous pressures of the big fellows who flaunt them openly, knowing that slow court procedures and small penalties make taking a chance eminently worthwhile.

Moreover fair trade laws, up until now, have been upheld in the courts only if a contract has been signed between the manufacturer or distributor and the retail dealer.

The proposed federal quality stabilization law would make such price maintenance on branded goods universal. Providing that a manufacturer entered into such a resale price agreement with one dealer in a state, then all "nonsigners" in the state would be equally bound not knowingly to sell the same merchandise for less than the price stipulated.

We badly need such a law and we need it now. The small, independent businessman must have his right to compete guarded against the unrestrained, cutthroat competition and retaliatory price-cutting of large chain and department stores, and mail-order and discount houses. These establishments have been flourishing as a direct result of the breakdown of state resale price-maintenance laws.

Moreover the manufacturer who has put so much effort, money, and ingenuity into the research, manufacture, and advertising of a branded product should be allowed to protect his investment.

Finally, the consumer will benefit from federal fair trade legislation. The chains and discount houses naturally oppose resale price maintenance, claiming that it would "penalize" them for their "more efficient distribution methods." The savings they make possible by their efficiency, they say, now go into the consumer's pocketbook; fair trade laws legislate against the consumer and are a device to assure the survival of the unfit.

Of course, price-cutting *might* give a short-run benefit to local consumers. On the other hand, it has been seen again and again that price-cutting on national brands is not done out of any loving concern for the consumer, but to lure people into the discount store. Once led in by a loss-leader, customers often pay a great deal more for the other items they purchase. Moreover the loss-leaders, especially if they are large items such as nationally branded appliances, often turn out to be "nailed to the floor." You go in and find that the famous-brand refrigerator offered at a ridiculously low price has been "sold out." Then a fast-talking salesman tries to turn your attention to less well-known brands which are "just as good."

Ethical merchants, who will not stoop to using such tactics against the consumer, need a law to protect them from unscrupulous discount houses. The quality stabilization bill, by permitting manufacturers to set a minimum price on national brands, would eliminate the use of such false lures to get customers into the stores.

Studies show that the abandonment of fair competitive practices does not mean any reduction in the average level of retail prices. There are some indications, indeed, that average prices decline when fair competitive practices are instituted.

One famous study by H. F. Ostlund and C. R. Vickland compared retail prices in a period of time (from March to September, 1939) when retail price maintenance was effective in most states, with a date immediately before price maintenance was introduced. Their research covered fifty well-known brands of items sold in drugstores in forty-eight states, and showed a 0.9 per cent average drop in the retail prices of these brands after fair competitive practices became effective. Chain stores tended to raise, and other stores to reduce, their prices.

It is obvious, too, that pricing is only one form of competition in retailing. This is often overlooked in debates concerning the wisdom of fair trade laws. What about service competition? Competition of location and convenience? Competition of personalities among the owners and employees of different stores? Advertising competition? Merchandising and inventory competition?

Of all these forms of competition—all extremely important to the consumer—opponents of fair trade laws stress only the loss of price competition. And the evidence is that even price competition will be much healthier if fair trade is made possible by legislation.

In the debate over fair trade laws to protect the small retailers, one is liable to overlook the serious social questions involved in the controversy. The vast majority of American small businessmen are retail merchants. Here, in the retail business sector, are the people who provide the community responsibility and leadership. The local druggist, the hardware merchant, the photo-dealer—these are the people who take pride in their community and serve it with their time, energy, and money.

Local retail stores also support thousands of families throughout the country. Like the family farm, the family business offers an ideal climate for the development of good qualities of character and morality. The energy-demanding work of the family store virtually eliminates juvenile delinquency. Qualities of thrift, industry, and business sense are developed and nurtured in the family atmosphere. Thus the family store is an immensely valuable American institution. It must be preserved.

Even if the family retail store were an economically inefficient operation, its contribution to family and community would be a strong enough argument in favor of its preservation. But like the family farm, it has proven itself efficient again and again. It lacks, however, one important asset for survival in our competitive economy —capital. This means that the large competitor, the chain store or discount house, even if less efficient, can engage in price-cutting operations until the little business is driven out of the market.

Cutthroat competition against the small businessman is increasing. The trend is toward more and bigger discount chains. While the pricing policies of the discount houses have a deceptive attractiveness, the long-range result is almost certain to be reduced competition, greater economic concentration, and higher prices.

Quality stabilization legislation is a sound way to insure that we will continue to have diversification and competition in retailing in the strengthening of the small business community. By the time you read this, such legislation may have been enacted. I intend to work hard for its passage.

Can You Sell Abroad?

17

IS THE NEW WORLD MARKET
FOR YOU?

The *bomberos* (fire-fighters) of Concepción, Chile, are all pretty envious of Fire Company 3, off the main plaza. Just like firemen the world over, Chilean *bomberos* are keen rivals in such matters as getting to the fire in the quickest time, keeping up the swash and sparkle of the individual fireman, and, most of all, competing for the largest, shiniest, and best-equipped firetrucks.

The men of Company 3 recently bought two big, new firetrucks manufactured by the Central Fire Truck Corporation of Manchester, Missouri. The trucks easily outshine anything else going to a fire in the whole of Chile.

For the little Missouri firm, too, the Chilean sale was a proud event. Central Fire Truck employs twenty-seven people, who design and build firetrucks to individual specifications on Dodge or General Motors bodies. Two years ago Otto Erker and Harry Nash, Central's executive heads, decided expansion was imperative.

On the domestic market, turnover on such items as firetrucks is understandably slight. Central's firetrucks are built to last for years, and home competition is keen.

"It was tough to know where to begin," Harry Nash says now. "Then a foreign trade counselor working out of SBA's St. Louis office, Tory Orest, suggested the possibility of exporting.

"We were pretty dubious. We felt that a small company, located smack in the middle of the country, wouldn't have a chance in exporting."

However, Otto and Harry decided to follow up at least one SBA suggestion. They sent their advertising brochures and prices to importers of fire-fighting equipment throughout the world, using trade lists supplied as a regular service by the U.S. Department of Commerce.

"As a result of this mailing, Concepción now has two of our trucks—a $16,000 sale," Nash says. "What's more, we've since had a chance to bid on seven other orders from Chile."

After this initial success, Central was encouraged to ship a fire truck to the Damascus Trade Fair in Syria. Not only did this bring inquiries and several orders, including a contract from Bangkok to construct an airport crash truck for the Royal Thai Air Force, but at the close of the fair the Damascus Fire Department snapped up the Central truck.

"Having broken the ice," Nash says, "our firm is

well on the way towards developing new markets and sales for our products overseas."

The experience of Central Fire Truck Corporation has been repeated many times in the past few years, as more and more companies—many small businesses among them—are getting into the export business and making a go of it. A saturated market here in the United States for certain durable goods is a problem facing manufacturers of many products, not just firetrucks.

In addition to manufactured goods, we have many *services* which are highly exportable: engineering skills, city planning and rural development know-how, and agricultural and technical skills. These certainly should not be overlooked in any discussion of exports.

Nor should we fall into the trap of thinking that only big businesses are in a position to export. Central Fire Truck is only one of the small firms successfully dealing in the export market. Another excellent example is W. G. Hunt, Inc., of Laurinberg, North Carolina, recipient of one of the President's "E" awards for export expansion, presented to six small businessmen in 1962.

Hunt manufactures a semi-automatic tipping and collating machine which printers use to produce snap-out business forms. Exports, now being shipped to eighteen countries, represent 35 per cent of Hunt's total business.

And the amazing part of this story is that Hunt does it all by himself! "My domestic and export departments run very smoothly," he says. "I handle all advertising, ordering, manufacturing, quality control, sales, shipping, billing, payroll—and the broom. I'm a one-man business."

There are many reasons—urgent reasons—why the small manufacturing and service concern should think hard about the possibilities in export.

There are certainly many problems and pitfalls in the export business, both in getting started and staying in. It is my conviction, however, that export is a wide open field for the firm that is aggressive, flexible, and willing to take advantage of the available advice and assistance.

First, let's look at the over-all picture, keeping in mind that everything I say presupposes that you have a product or a service for which there's a market overseas, a product you can sell at a fair profit.

Today, to an increasing extent—whether we'd prefer to ignore it or not—the market place is becoming worldwide. Huge regional trading areas—the European Common Market, the Outer Seven, the Latin American Free Trade Area, the move toward creating a unified Central America—show the trend. Old barriers that used to stop goods—imports and exports—at the frontiers are rapidly breaking down.

To permit American goods to go into these great trading blocs, Congress recently passed the far-reaching Trade Expansion Act, giving the President authority to lower and adjust tariffs on goods coming into this country in return for concessions that permit American exports to move into European and other trading areas.

Foreign competition: the negative side

Now, the other side of the coin: foreign competition in this country. It's tough now in many lines, and it's going to get tougher—in some commodities much tougher. The hard fact is that some businesses either must improve their products and methods drastically to stay alive—perhaps even adapt their production facilities to new lines—or go out of business.

Under the new Trade Expansion Act, there also will be "adjustment insurance" administered by SBA for any businesses directly affected by the lower tariffs on foreign goods. But I'd like to defer a more complete discussion of the Trade Act and other assists from Uncle Sam to the next chapter. Right now, I want to stress the positive side.

The new world market

The smart businessman—large or small—will look at the export picture in terms of the emerging world market, with its millions and millions of potential customers. Americans, busy pushing out from the great New England manufacturing centers to the West and South, have concentrated on the great American market, leaving the rest of the world to a relatively few American enterprisers.

Why? High tariffs (or downright exclusion of U.S.-made products), as well as difficulties of communication and transportation, have been big obstacles. And, manufacturers could sell everything they produced right here at home. Also, we are not particularly concerned with the world market right now. Of 318,000 U.S. manufacturing firms, only 12,000 sell beyond the domestic scene. Only 4 per cent of the United States' gross national product is sent abroad, and the small business participation in this limited amount of export is infinitesimal.

Now, however, with instantaneous communications and trade barriers crashing everywhere, a world market becomes inevitable. And trade barriers are falling at exactly the moment when the American market is surfeited with certain lines of goods.

The world-market is opening up when the prestige of American goods—the label "Made in USA"—has never been higher. In country after country, as basic needs of food, clothing, and shelter are satisfied, people are looking to the U.S. for the consumer goods they associate with the "good life" we've built here—and they have the money to pay for them.

What concrete advantages in export?

In general, international trade activity tends to benefit the domestic economy in terms of *more* sales and *more* employment. For example, two firetrucks might mean the difference between a good year and an indifferent one to Central Fire Truck Corporation. That in itself is important enough.

But one $2 million plane purchased by a Latin American air line means orders for no less than 2,000 U.S. firms, including a whopping $590,000 for small businesses on subcontracts. All up and down the scale, then, for big businesses and for small, export may—more and more—mean the difference between profit and deficit when the year's sales are added up.

A manufacturer, large or small, already has fixed expenses in his domestic production; extra units for overseas sales can be so much low-cost gravy. Moreover, exporting can be a solution for disposing of domestic oversupply, or can help "cushion" a business over dips in the U.S. economy. There seems to be a six-month lag in recessions overseas, and by the time the downturn affects the overseas buyers, domestic customers are sending in the orders again.

Profitable? With expert assistance and the right product, small businesses in one instance after another are selling abroad and, in three to five years, realizing a full return on the capital, after taxes. Some small businessmen, indeed, feel that entry into export is not a choice but a necessity for survival, that it is a case of export or expire.

Bob Hood, president of the Ansul Chemical Company in Marinette, Wisconsin, has brought growth and rejuvenation to his whole community by insisting that his company sell abroad.

"I have made a statement in our company repeatedly," he says, "and I have no reason to change it at this time. I have said that if we as a company are not an international company in the next ten years, our chances of growth are materially reduced and our survival is jeopardized."

Here is a man with a truly international approach and a positive vision of the world-market. "There are some terms that bother me a little," he says. "The term 'abroad.' The term 'foreign.' If you adopt the view that you are an international company, nothing is 'foreign' or 'alien' or 'abroad.' The world is your market, and you must learn how to deal in a larger market place and be an economic and social part of it."

Uncle Sam's balance of payments

The whole question of export has another positive aspect. When you go into export, providing you have a product that can be successfully marketed abroad and make a fair profit for you, you're helping the U.S. in the big balance of payments problem.

We've been seriously lagging behind in the kind of exporting that brings dollars flowing back into our own economy. If we import more than we export, we put a serious drain on our gold reserves and endanger our whole domestic economic structure.

From Uncle Sam's point of view, U.S. exports have to increase or the economy will suffer. Our deficit situation is improving, but we must export roughly $2 billion more to reach a "break even" point.

Problems in the world-market

In a certain sense, our pump-priming foreign aid after World War II has been "too successful." Economies in Europe that recovered through Marshall Plan aid as well as the new economies sparked through Point IV and other technical and dollar assistance now are beginning to put out products directly competitive with those "Made in USA." But they are also developing rich markets for American goods. They are customers as well as competitors.

Our technical know-how is still the best in the world. Our goods have the reputation of being of high quality and durable. Our production and management practices are superior. And we've refined customer services and distribution methods to the level of high arts. With all these assets, there is no reason to fear that in the long run the United States will not be able to do more than hold her own.

But we have a big, added reason to hurry up our exports, for the Communist bloc is beginning to move its goods into many areas, particularly the newly developing nations.

Admittedly we have a tough fight ahead, because there is evidence that the Iron Curtain countries will go to almost any lengths to establish trade with these new nations. Harry Smith, who set up an export–import firm with offices in Milwaukee and Naples, recently had personal experience with a vicious "price war" being waged against U.S. and Canadian exports to Italy.

"I am leaving Italy after six months of striving to combat the extreme measures being used by some of the countries behind the Iron Curtain to place products in Europe," he wrote me recently. "The products men-

171

tioned are of a superior quality and, I might add, of such a ridiculously low price level as to insure no competition whatsoever with certain products from the United States and Canada. It seems that they are willing to go to such measures as offering these same products at less than cost to attract business and start trade with these countries, so as to undermine trade with us."

But Communist economic assistance comes with strings—economic dependence is the first step towards political takeover. Our goods, therefore, not only can make profits for us and help Uncle Sam balance his world-trade accounts, but they also are powerful ammunition in the cold war we are fighting today: the war for freedom.

18

WILL UNCLE SAM HELP YOU
SELL ABROAD?

However successful some small businesses are
becoming in the export field, there are still many difficulties facing the man who wants to send his product
or service overseas. Success in export is by no means
automatic. Some small companies have gone into export and have lost everything they put into the venture.

I hope, however, that I've said enough to convince
you that export is a promising area for the small
businessman. If he has a good product and is willing
to research his market and give good service, he has a
chance of making a profit—sometimes a big one—and
contributing to the general economic health of the
U. S. as well.

In this chapter, I want to examine the steps the
prospective small exporter must take—and the difficulties he must face squarely—one by one. With each step
I'll have something to say about the assistance available to you, both from government and from private
sources.

But before going into this step-by-step description of the export process, it is necessary to set the stage by describing what is probably the biggest assist of the decade for businessmen who plan to expand to new markets overseas: The Trade Expansion Act of 1962.

During these next few years, you're going to be hearing a great deal about the Trade Expansion Act and its effect on American business. The act, designed primarily to encourage American exports and thus help reverse the chronic balance of payments difficulties we've been suffering during the past few years, was considered first-priority legislation, and the Administration labored mightily to push the bill through Congress.

The act will encourage the European Common Market and the other important trading countries and blocs with which we deal—Canada, Japan, Latin America—to lower their trade barriers so that more American goods can reach these booming new overseas markets. In spite of some reservations I still have about it, I think that, on the whole, it's a good bill.

Very simply, the act permits the President to cut American tariffs as much as 50 per cent on most goods in return for the same trade concessions from other countries and from the free trade areas. The Trade Expansion Act gives us a great advantage, in that we now have a tool to make deals on whole classes of goods in very large trading areas, instead of having to make painful, product-by-product negotiations with separate countries.

When President Kennedy signed the bill in October, 1962, he called it "the most important international piece of legislation since the passage of the Marshall Plan."

> "We cannot protect our economy by stagnating behind high tariff walls. The best protection possible is a mutual lowering of tariff barriers among friendly nations so that all may benefit from a free flow of goods."

The new Trade Expansion Act was first used to bargain with the six Common Market nations in May, 1962. A conference (at which Christian A. Herter, President Kennedy's chief tariff negotiator, headed the U. S. delegation) laid down so-called "ground rules" for the May, 1964, world-wide tariff negotiations, to be held under the auspices of the General Agreement on Tariffs and Trade (GATT). In GATT, the U. S. and sixty-six other countries have joined together, under United Nations auspices, to cut world-wide tariffs and foster the liberalization of trade.

The U. S. won a major concession during these preliminary tariff negotiations. The French wanted a formula which would have cut high U. S. tariffs by half, but would have left some lower European tariffs as they were—to correct what some of the Europeans regarded as "basic inequities." But the U. S. formula, a flat 50 per cent cut for everyone on broad categories of goods, prevailed.

The Trade Expansion Act was needed. The Common Market provides a kind of trading opportunity that has never existed before in the history of world trade, and its rate of growth already is one-half higher than the current U. S. growth rate. We need to export in order to close that gap.

Moreover, we're now in a good position so far as the European Common Market is concerned. Our exports are about 50 per cent higher than our imports from ECM members.

On the darker side, it is of course inevitable that trade liberalization is going to mean difficult adjustments for some of our industries. Many of those which will be hit—and hit hard—will be small businesses, especially if they are not flexible enough to adapt and diversify their lines, anticipate competition, and go all out for export themselves if they have a suitable product.

The Trade Expansion Act itself gives the President authority to assist those industries, firms, and workers who may be seriously injured by the increased imports resulting from trade agreements. Some imports have been put on a reserved list, and the import duty will not be lowered on them. Others have been placed on a provisional list and, in the event of injury, an application to have them put on the reserved list may be made to the U. S. Tariff Commission.

The Tariff Commission also is required by the act to advise the President on the probable economic implication of any proposed trade concession before it goes into effect. Six months prior to any negotiations, the President provides the Tariff Commission a list of products on which he plans to negotiate. The commission then sets up hearings, and all interested persons have an opportunity to be heard for or against the particular concessions. The President also consults his other executive departments—Commerce, Labor, Agriculture—on negotiation questions.

Finding your market

How can you get into the rich export market? There is no blanket formula for finding your proper market. Each product and manufacturing situation is different, and you can't be sure that any single approach will always work.

First make sure that the market in which you're interested is suitable for your particular product. One truck manufacturer was all set to sell transport trucks in a country which boasted less than 100 miles of paved roads! Such trucks, obviously, would not be of any use there for at least ten years.

Perhaps a steady increase in unsolicited orders from certain areas will tip you off on where to start. Indeed, increasing orders from overseas often provide just the push small manufacturers need to get into export in an organized way.

Among the publications which can help you find markets are the United States Bureau of the Census *Foreign Trade Reports* (Series FT 420), available from the Department of Commerce. From these you can determine, commodity by commodity, just how many of what goods are being purchased from U. S. firms by some 160 countries. By comparing month-to-month and year-to-year statistics for your product, you can judge which markets are expanding most rapidly. United Nations *Commodity Trade Statistics,* issued monthly, will provide valuable supplementary information.

After you've chosen an export area, it would be advisable for you to go yourself to look over the new situation, if this is at all possible. It is most important for top management in a small company, at least in the beginning, to know the foreign situation at first hand.

"I learned from bumps on my head," says Bob Hood of Ansul Chemical, whom I introduced in the last chapter. "I tried to delegate the leg-work in connection with an operation Ansul has in Mexico. It didn't work out at all. Just a couple of months ago we finally got out from under and back to the spot we should have started on. We lost about two years, but perhaps we learn through these trials."

Another good way to analyze your new market—nearly as effective as going yourself—is to find a specialist who knows the area and understands your product. Then trust him, retaining, of course, the policy decisions for yourself.

There are many aids in analyzing the prospective market, either to supplement a personal, on-the-spot visit or to substitute for firsthand inspection.

The U. S. Department of Commerce probably is the greatest single source of information for the would-be exporter. As I mentioned earlier, a massive overhauling is going on in the department, and its interest in export has been rapidly intensified as a result of Commerce's belief that domestic and foreign marketing are becoming indivisible. International market programs now are concentrated in the new Bureau of International Commerce.

In addition to its thirty-four field offices, which will counsel you in person, the Department of Commerce has a number of publications. These include *International Commerce* (a weekly devoted to developments in world trade, changes in trade regulations, and trade opportunities) and *Overseas Business Reports* (some 250 are published annually, dealing in depth with such subjects as markets for U. S. products in Vietnam, manufacturing in Greece, Pakistan's licensing and exchange controls, and the like). Then there are Commerce *Trade Lists* (giving names and addresses of principal foreign manufacturers, processors, wholesalers, and distributors' sales agents, grouped by commodity, as well as the names of those who perform certain services, which cost one dollar per country.

Recent *Trade Lists* cover such things as architects, builders, contractors, and engineers in Portugal, business firms in Gibraltar, dry goods and clothing importers and dealers in Pakistan, hardware importers and dealers in Peru, and fish and vegetable oil importers and dealers in South Africa. A check list of all the publications available can be obtained from the Bureau of International Commerce.

The New Orleans Metal Company (in spite of the name, the firm deals in waste paper and wiping cloth) was able, through *Trade Lists,* to send out letters to pulp and paper mills all over the world.

"Within a year and a half we were able to increase the volume of our business by about 30 per cent," Ken Plunkett, New Orleans Metal head says. "We are very optimistic about our exporting. We see no reason why it should not continue."

Many other publications and counseling services are offered by the Department of Commerce to businessmen interested in export. The department will send you descriptions of other assistance on request. You should especially look into such aids as participation in U. S. trade missions, which explain your product and put potential buyers in touch with you, as well as give you the chance to exhibit at U. S. trade fairs abroad and at permanent trade centers in various countries, which Central Fire Truck used so successfully. Of the 60 initial exhibitors at the new Tokyo trade center, opened in spring, 1962, 30 were small businesses, and 13 of these were encouraged to exhibit on the initiative of SBA. Since the trade fairs program was inaugurated in 1954, 4,000 U. S. firms have displayed and demonstrated their products at 127 exhibits in 29 countries.

For a nominal fee, American foreign service officials will prepare, on request from the Department of Commerce, what are called "country reports," tailored to your own needs, and giving vital information about any particular country on such matters as population, the labor situation, standard of living, possible competitors, and the like. The officials also attempt to locate three or four local firms interested in your product.

Finally, the Agency for International Development has a small business division ready to assist manufacturers of many lines of manufactured goods needed in newly developing areas. SBA's foreign trade division will also help.

You can obtain useful information to supplement these sources from chambers of commerce, commercial banks and mercantile trust agencies, and transportation companies. The Pan American *Clipper Cargo Horizons,* for example, publishes a regular listing of world wide marketing opportunities, and will also publicize your product free of charge.

Starting out

Once you've decided on the countries you'd like to export to, and have investigated the market opportunities, you're ready to consider the method of export best-suited to your company and your product.

Two obvious courses open to big companies generally are out for the small businessman. You usually can't afford to set up your own export department, nor can you solve your problem by building a whole new factory overseas.

Yours is the indirect method of working with and through others, at least for the first few years. You might choose the obvious method of marketing through an export agent or a commission house. But there are more interesting channels, which may provide a lasting foundation for overseas expansion.

The combination export firm offers one of the best means of starting out. These firms act, in many ways, like your own export department, even writing customers on your company letterhead. Most CEM's these days take all the risks; that is, they buy your product outright and then resell it overseas. Thus the shipping, insurance, credit, and collecting—and the headaches—are all theirs.

However, businessmen tell me that a word of caution is in order here. There are 600 to 1,000 CEM's operating today, and as few as 300 are competent and reliable.

The joint venture is another possibility, a step that has led to some very profitable business abroad. Taking on an overseas partner may, in some cases, not be a matter of choice but of necessity in the nationalistic, rapidly developing areas of the world. Already there are laws in some countries requiring that a certain number of employees at the executive level be from the country itself. A partnership gets around many of the difficulties of being an "imperialistic Yankee" company in countries not always so understanding about the way our economic system has evolved since the turn of the century. Best of all, of course, local partners are in an excellent position to know local conditions, customers, and product potential.

Contract manufacturing and licensing are still other methods, depending on whether your product lends itself to outright manufacture by an overseas producer.

If you're shipping direct—

The information on markets and manufacture outlined above will be of use to you only when you've decided to take the plunge—with both feet—into the overseas market.

If you're still in a stage of indecision and not yet ready to go quite that far, there are many aids available to you in shipping direct, either to facilitate your filling of unsolicited orders or to help you begin marketing in a modest way from your own home base.

Concise information on credit and methods of payment, for example, is available in a new Department of Commerce publication, *Exporting: A How-To-Get-Started Handbook.* Other guides and information sheets are available from such sources as the foreign trade division of SBA or the foreign department of your nearest international bank. And if you need credit information on a specific customer ordering from abroad, you may find it in Commerce's *World Trade Directory Reports,* which outlines the business reputation of thousands of overseas firms.

Insurance on shipments overseas has been a serious problem, because underwriting of guarantees against political risks was difficult to obtain. One firm overextended ninety-day credit on exports to Argentina, and then faced serious financial difficulties when dollar reserves were frozen for three years and no payment could be sent out of the country.

Now, however, after considerable pressure from the

business community and legislators interested in making export more attractive to businessmen, the Export–Import bank, in cooperation with the Federal Credit Insurance Association, early last year widened its services to granting policies covering transactions involving political risks such as wars, revolutions, freezing of currency, and so on. This is in contrast to former, higher-priced comprehensive policies which covered both political and credit risks in cases where the commercial risk was slight. The new insurance rates on commercial risks also are more reasonable in price.

Finally, there are even helps in preparing your goods for shipment. The Department of Commerce publishes a series of pamphlets titled *Preparing Shipments to* [*name of country*]. Some 150 different countries are covered, and the pamphlets give import regulations, rules for labeling and marking, and customs procedures.

If you've come along with me this far on the subject of exporting, you may be willing to admit that exporting is a pretty good idea in the abstract, but "not for me."

Admittedly, there are still many difficulties in going abroad. Some of these the small businessman (and the large one) brings on himself. There is often a tendency to slack off on quality and efficiency when the foreign orders come in, perhaps letting orders lie on the desk because of lack of initiative in finding out shipping and customs regulations, or because the letters and orders arrive in another language and no one in the small firm is able to read them.

Or perhaps a shipment of goods is sent that is not quite up to par—a great mistake, businessmen tell me, quite apart from the question of business integrity involved. Japan, West Germany, and the Communist bloc countries are pursuing aggressive export policies, and they're manufacturing and shipping top-quality goods to overseas markets. Any falling off in the quality of American goods will simply result in loss of future orders.

In spite of the difficulties, however, I firmly believe that the export field offers the far-seeing and imaginative businessman a new frontier which has, until now, remained virtually unexplored. The chances are that you will be missing out on a big opportunity if you fail at least to investigate your chances to market your products or services overseas.

Will Congress Go To Bat
For You?

19

WILL THE GOVERNMENT EASE
THAT TAX BURDEN?

An automobile dealer in a small Wisconsin town has been in business for about fifteen years. He employed a regular bookkeeper, who kept his business records, and he hired an accountant in his home town to prepare his tax returns.

When, two years ago, the bookkeeper died and the accountant moved out of state to secure better employment, the dealer decided to hire someone to keep his books and take care of his tax problems as well. He secured the services of a young man who had just graduated from a nearby junior college. The young man meant well and worked hard at his new job. However, he was too inexperienced to compute accurately the tax return for the company. After a routine inquiry from the Internal Revenue Service on several points in his return, the dealer had a professional audit—and discovered that he had overpaid his 1961 and 1962 taxes by some $3,500.

If up-to-date tax information and a clear, concise interpretation of Internal Revenue Service regulations had been available, this dealer's tax problems would not have been so difficult. What he needed was a person who could intelligently and accurately prepare his income tax in such a manner that the government would be paid what was rightfully coming to it, but who could also advise him on how to proceed in his business planning in order to take advantage of the tax benefits that are available under our present laws.

This same situation is, I am afraid, faced by many small businesses throughout the country. Not only have their taxes grown in dollars but the regulations have grown more complicated with the years.

Small businessmen have more difficulty than any other class of taxpayer in coping with the complexities and inequities of our tax structure, both in terms of the Internal Revenue Code itself and also in its administration by the Internal Revenue Service.

The revenue code is so complex, especially in those sections which relate to business, that the average small businessman cannot understand it. This places the small company at a disadvantage in preparing its returns, in tax planning, and in the audit of its returns by the Internal Revenue Service. Despite the continuing and sincere efforts of the Internal Revenue Service to avoid disparity of treatment and to be helpful to taxpayers in auditing procedures, a small company without expert advice is at a disadvantage on many issues, such as depreciation, accumulation of earnings, and travel and entertainment expenses.

As a businessman, you are a taxpayer as well as a tax collector for your city, state, and nation.

The number of federal taxes alone that you must handle is formidable. First, you are responsible for the payment of a federal income tax on the income of your business and your family. Often you must also make quarterly payments of estimated tax, supply information returns with regard to the payment of wages, interest, and dividends, withhold income tax and social security taxes from the wages of your employees, pay your company's share of social security and unemployment insurance taxes, and, in many cases, keep detailed records in connection with the collection of federal excise taxes.

State and local jurisdictions levy many other taxes on you which require responsible attention.

If your small business were a large corporation, you could afford to hire trained experts to handle this tax problem. But you find yourself facing the bewildering variety of taxes yourself. These duties occupy time and energy that you would otherwise use in more vital management tasks. And failure to comply with tax regulations can spell trouble for you.

Existing tax rates are more burdensome if you are a small, growing concern than if you are a large, well-established enterprise. Since investment capital is so hard for you to obtain, your ability to accumulate earnings to finance further expansion is particularly important. For this reason alone, taxes on your earnings are especially burdensome.

If you are organized as a corporation, you do receive some relief from the surtax exemption. This provision exempts the first $25,000 of your corporate net income from the 26 per cent surtax. On earnings below this level, you must still pay the normal tax of 22 per cent, however, and the effective rate of tax rises rapidly toward the combined maximum of 48 per cent as your earnings increase beyond $25,000. When your net income is $50,000, for example, your effective tax rate is 35 per cent; when your earnings are $100,000, your rate is 41.5 per cent.

Here, too, the large organization can get a better break. A large enterprise organized as a number of separate corporate units under common control can receive the benefit of multiple surtax exemptions, while retaining many of the economic advantages of a large concern.

The federal estate tax, while justified on the grounds of broad social policy, presents you with estate planning problems so serious that you may be tempted to merge your firm with a larger one rather than attempt to pass its control on to your heirs. You must insure that your estate will have the cash necessary to meet any estate tax liability. This is clearly a problem if you have invested your efforts and capital in a single business enterprise. If your estate does not have sufficient liquidity to meet the tax, your heirs may find it necessary to sell—perhaps at distress prices—a substantial interest in your business. On the other hand, if you set aside earnings in anticipation of estate tax liabilities, you cannot invest it in the growth of the firm.

Certain provisions in the Technical Amendments Act of 1958 have helped alleviate this problem. In particular, one provision permits installment payments over a ten-year period, when the estate consists largely of a closely held business. But difficulties persist, particularly over the valuation of the business for estate tax purposes. Often there is no basis for a reasonable evaluation of a closely held business, especially if the stock is not traded in an organized market. Also, so much may have depended on the ability of the deceased owner; past profits may bear little relation to what the business can actually be sold for after the founder's death.

The situation is often made worse by the fear that Internal Revenue agents will tend to overvalue the business for estate tax purposes. Although such fear is unfounded, it intensifies the uncertainty surrounding estate planning.

All too often the final result is the merger of a small, growing concern with a larger one.

Below, I give you an explanation of the provisions of the federal income tax laws that are of special significance to small business firms. There are, of course, other sections in the code that apply to business, but the ones I give should be given most consideration by small business. The detailed analysis of these provisions may provide a check list for you in evaluating your present tax-return procedures.

President Kennedy, in January, 1963, proposed to Congress a broad tax revision program. The bill based on these proposals has now been enacted. The major changes in the bill which affect small business are also given at the end of the chapter.

In setting priorities for federal tax relief, small business should certainly be at the top of the list. However, those who want to change the federal tax laws should be charged with showing that such changes would clearly and positively benefit small business. I would certainly not be willing to suggest that Congress trifle with the tax laws unless there is a clear showing of substantial benefit to all within the small business community.

Key provisions of the federal tax code affecting small business

1. Under subchapter "S" of the Internal Revenue Code (Sec. 1371–1377), a closely held domestic corporation may elect not to be taxed as a corporation. All of the shareholders must give their consent, and upon such election the corporation is taxed as if it were a partnership. In order to qualify, the corporation must have ten or fewer stockholders, all of whom must either be individuals or estates. Certain other require-

ments set forth in subchapter "S" must also be met. Generally speaking, if the individual shareholder's tax rates are about the same as, or less than, the rate of tax imposed on a corporation's income, it would appear advisable to make this election.

2. Under Sec. 1244 of the code, an individual may take an ordinary loss deduction of up to $25,000 on losses sustained on the sale or worthlessness of stock issued by a small business corporation as defined in Sec. 1244. The stock must have been issued in accordance with a plan adopted by the small business corporation subsequent to June 30, 1958, and must meet other requirements set forth in Sec. 1244.

3. Estates taxes: a) Under Sec. 6161, upon the finding of undue hardship by the Secretary of the Treasury or his delegate, the time for payment of estate taxes may be extended for periods of up to ten years. Any unpaid tax bears interest at 4 per cent per annum. As a practical matter, extensions are granted for only one year at a time.

b) Under Sec. 6166, when an interest in a closely held business (as defined in the section) constitutes either 35 per cent of the taxpayer's gross estate or 50 per cent of the taxable estate, the executor may elect to pay the estate tax in two or more, but not more than ten, equal annual installments. Here again, the unpaid tax bears interest at 4 per cent per annum.

4. Under Sec. 179, a taxpayer may deduct an additional 20 per cent first-year depreciation allowance on tangible personal property purchased during the year.

This 20 per cent bonus depreciation deduction applies to both new and used property. It was made applicable to used property in order to be available to small firms, which usually have to buy the less expensive used equipment. The maximum deduction allowed under the section is $10,000.

5. Under Sec. 46, which was enacted as a part of the Revenue Act of 1962, the 7 per cent investment credit is made available on investment up to $50,000 in used assets. This was included in the Revenue Act of 1962 for the reasons outlined above with regard to the 20 per cent first-year depreciation allowance.

6. SBICs: a) Sec. 243(b) of the Internal Revenue Code provides that SBICs may deduct from their otherwise taxable income 100 per cent of the dividends they receive on stock acquired from domestic small business concerns in which they invest.

b) Sec. 1242 of the code provides that a stockholder in an SBIC is entitled to an ordinary loss deduction rather than a capital loss, where a loss is incurred through the sale or exchange of the SBIC stock.

c) Sec. 1243 of the code permits an SBIC to take an ordinary loss deduction rather than a capital loss where it incurs a loss on the sale or exchange of a convertible debenture that it acquires from a small business concern, or on stock acquired through exercise of the conversion privilege. Contrary to popular belief, present tax law does not permit an SBIC to take an ordinary loss on any type of security except convertible debentures or stock acquired through exercise of the conversion privilege. Since enactment of the 1961 amendments, SBICs may acquire many other types of securities from small business concerns, but losses on them will be limited to capital loss treatment. For example, a loss on stock purchased directly from a small business concern will be treated as a capital loss, which can be offset only against capital gains. If the SBIC has no capital gains, then such a loss would be subject to the carryover provisions of the code.

d) Under Sec. 542 of the code, an SBIC is exempted from the personal holding-company surtax, as are banks, life insurance companies, as well as finance companies. However, the SBIC loses its exemption if one of its shareholders owns 5 per cent or more of a concern to which the SBIC provides funds. This qualification is certainly desirable, in that it serves to discourage self-dealing. However, the Internal Revenue Service has held that the attribution rules are applicable in applying the 5 per cent test. Under this ruling, where an SBIC takes a stock interest in a completely unrelated small business concern, this stock interest is attributed to the stockholders of the SBIC in proportion to their interest in the SBIC, and if the "attributed" interest of any one stockholder amounts to 5 per cent of the small concern, the SBIC loses its exemption. Obviously, such an SBIC has not engaged in self-dealing, but has merely done what it was intended to do, to provide equity capital to independent small business concerns.

President Kennedy's recommendations on reforms affecting small business, as enacted

1. Beginning in 1964, the President's plan reduces corporate tax rates. For companies with net incomes of $25,000 or less, the rate is lowered from 30 to 22 per cent. For corporations with net incomes above $25,000, the rate is reduced from 52 to 50 per cent in 1964, and will be further reduced to 48 per cent in 1965. The benefits of the immediate reduction on the first $25,000 of corporate income will represent a drop of 27 per cent in tax for corporations with $25,000 or less of net income.

2. The bill provides three alternatives for companies which have 80 per cent or more joint ownership. First, the group could continue to have multiple exemptions of $25,000 from surtax if each company were willing to pay an additional 6 per cent tax. Second, the group can file a consolidated return and have only one surtax exemption. Third, the members of the group can file a consolidated return and have only one surtax exemption. Third, the members of the group can file separate returns, forego multiple exemptions, and pay no tax on dividends distributed within the group.

3. The bill also provides individual income tax rate cuts. The reductions would be made over a two-year period, starting in 1964, and would scale down the present range of 20 to 91 per cent to 14 to 70 per cent.

4. Under another provision, a taxpayer can average his current income with that of the past four years,

and if current income amounts to more than 133 per cent of the average, he will be allowed, in effect, to treat the excess over 133 per cent as though it were earned over a five-year period. Thus he would be taxed at a considerably reduced rate. Since incomes of many small, unincorporated businesses are subject to wide fluctuations from year to year, their owners would especially benefit from the averaging provision.

20

CAN YOU GET A GOVERNMENT CONTRACT?

Gordon Spence operates an established, well-run machine shop in Wisconsin. He takes great pride in the precision of his work, which is highly praised by his customers. Business is good but he wants it to be better.

One obvious place for Spence to turn for an increase in business is the United States Government. He believes that he could fulfill some of the many defense contracts being awarded each year by the Department of Defense.

Spence decided to find out how to obtain a share in the government's business. He knew that he could not perform a large prime contract, but he was confident that he could handle—and handle well—a subcontract. After many inquiries, he found that the large prime contractors for the Defense Department did much of their contract "in house," subcontracting the rest to two small subcontractors over and over again.

Gordon Spence is not alone. Many other competent small businessmen and manufacturers, without the means to hire Washington representatives to keep them informed about what the government is buying, are losing out on government contract work which they can and should do.

Something must be done to see that Gordon Spence and other proprietors of small shops and plants get a fair opportunity to bid on important defense work.

I have held a series of government-contract opportunities conferences in Wisconsin. These meetings have been a revelation to many Wisconsin small businessmen. The government and prime contractors alike send out procurement officials who are looking for small businesses that can and will do a competent subcontracting job. And believe me, they are looking.

The federal government is by far the largest purchaser of goods and services in this country. It is vital to our economy and to small business that the latter provide its fair share of these goods and services. The government's spending on military needs and space this year—together with projected spending—defies the imagination. It is hard for most of us, concerned with payments on our house or car, to comprehend the billions of dollars that are involved in these programs.

The budget submitted by the President for fiscal year 1964 provides for the expenditure of $16,350,000,000 for the purchase of weapons and military equipment, $11,690,000,000 for the operation and maintenance of equipment and facilities, $7,120,000,000 for research and development, and $1,380,000,000 for military and related construction.* Expenditures in fiscal 1964 for civilian space programs are estimated at $4.2 billion, an increase of 75 per cent over 1963. *Fortune* magazine estimates that this amount will reach $20 billion by 1970.

Small business participation in this government spending has not been great. With 95 per cent of the firms and 40 per cent of the employment, the high point of small business participation in defense prime contract awards was 25.3 per cent in fiscal 1954. This percentage has declined each year until fiscal 1961, when it had fallen to 15.9 per cent. In fiscal 1962, 100 of the largest corporations received 72.3 per cent of the net value of military prime contract awards made by the Department of Defense.

The procurement techniques of the Defense Department are very important, since Defense is responsible for 80 per cent of all government purchases. (Small business does well in securing procurement contracts from the other major government buyer, the General Services Administration.)

President Kennedy recognized the failure of the Defense Department to procure a fair share of contracts from small business. He asked the Department of Defense to increase small business's share of defense

---

* Three out of every four dollars that the Department of Defense spends on prime contracts for work done in the United States are for hard goods (aircraft, ships, etc.), including related research and development. The remaining money is spent for soft goods (petroleum, textiles, etc.) and services.

prime contracts by 10 per cent. This was accomplished in fiscal 1962, bringing the percentage for this year to 17.7 per cent. The percentage for the first nine months of fiscal 1963, however, declined to 15.8 per cent. All indicators point to a failure to retain the 10 per cent increase this year.

The explanation for this given by the Department of Defense is based on the complexity of our modern weapons, and the "weapons system" type of military procurement. In weapons system procurement, one prime contract is let by the government for the design and production of a particular military item, such as a fighter plane or a bomber.

There is also a trend to fewer and bigger contracts in our space program. Most of the prime contractors on these space contracts, however, as well as weapons system contractors, will subcontract a large percentage of their awards. This subcontracting potential is of great interest to small business. It represents the best way for small business to increase its participation in defense procurement.

On September 26, 1961, a small business subcontracting program became law. The story of this law is a long and involved one. The law does not meet what those of us who wrote and fought for its adoption feel is required for a strong, effective subcontracting program. It represents only the beginning effort to assure that a fair share of the government's procurement dollar goes to small business.

The recognized need for more subcontracts for small business prompted Senator John Sparkman of Alabama, Chairman of the Senate Select Committee on Small Business, to introduce this bill, S. 2032, on May 21, 1959. This bill provided that it should be the policy of the government to award a fair proportion of contracts and subcontracts for property and services to small business enterprises. Under the bill, government contracting agencies would have been required to furnish the Small Business Administration with more complete procurement records. SBA would have been permitted access to procurement negotiation and award-board material. The bill would also have extended the small business set-aside program to subcontracts.

The bill, however, met with immediate Department of Defense disapproval. The department stated that the bill was an unnecessary and unjustified interference with its procurement responsibilities.

Hearings were held on this and other small business bills by the Small Business Subcommittee of the Senate Banking and Currency Committee in June and July, 1959. I was and still am chairman of this subcommittee. As a result of these hearings, the subcommittee reported a new bill to the full committee, one containing the Sparkman provisions (with some exceptions) along with a new provision which would have established a small business subcontracting program.

This subcontracting amendment was suggested to Senator A. Willis Robertson, Chairman of the Senate

Banking and Currency Committee, by Philip McCallum, then Administrator of the Small Business Administration. In commenting on the provision to extend the set-aside program to subcontracts, McCallum said in a letter that legislation establishing minimum standards for a subcontracting program was the best way for small business to achieve a fair proportion of subcontracts. I worked with the committee staff and with SBA to develop suitable legislative language for such a program.

After several technical revisions, the full committee unanimously reported the bill, with amendments, to the Senate on July 27, 1960. Section 8 of the bill, as reported by the committee, gave the administrator of SBA authority, after consultation with the assistant secretary of defense (supply and logistics), and the administrator of the General Services Administration, to initiate a small business subcontracting program.

This program would have insured that small business concerns would participate equitably as prime contractors and subcontractors in government procurement contracts, that the prime contractors and subcontractors would consult with and use the services and facilities of SBA when requested by SBA to do so, and that SBA could obtain from prime contractors and subcontractors such information and records on subcontracts as it might require. These requirements were to be included in every prime contract above $1 million, and in every subcontract above $500,000.

The committee report on the bill, in describing the new program, stated:

> This program will permit the Small Business Administration to have information available to it upon which to base intelligent suggestions to contractors as to qualified small businesses available to perform subcontracts. The program would not, and it is not the intent of the committee that it should, authorize the Small Business Administration to dictate to the contractor the extent to which he should make subcontracts or the persons to whom the subcontracts should be granted. The role of the Small Business Administration will be confined to furnishing information and suggestions.

Section 8 passed the Senate unanimously! But then the opposition really went to work. The Pentagon pressured the House conferees to kill the amendment. I was chairman of the Senate conferees when we met with House conferees several times to consider the amendment. We pressed the House hard for the amendment, but it failed to be reported out of that conference because of a tie vote on the part of the House conferees.

After the adjournment of the 86th Congress, Senator Sparkman, Senator Capehart, and I had several conferences with SBA and Pentagon officials in an effort to reach an understanding. Our main purpose was to give SBA, the agency established by Congress to foster and protect the interest of the small businessman, an effective voice in establishing a satisfactory procurement policy for small business.

At the beginning of the 87th Congress I introduced S. 836. The section of this bill establishing the proposed subcontracting program reflected our efforts to meet the major objections to the previous amendment. It was clearly stated that the program would not prescribe the extent to which any contractor should enter into contracts nor specify the business concerns to which subcontracts should be granted.

Shortly after the introduction of the bill, the Banking and Currency Committee was deluged with telegrams from private individuals and firms. Some unknown source had spread erroneous information regarding the bill and had stirred up very active opposition to it.

The impression left by the opposition's campaign was that the bill would set the administrator of the Small Business Administration up as the procurement czar of the country. It was alleged, in effect, that he would work his will on all procurement and override the wishes of the President, the Secretary of Defense, the administrator of General Services, and the Congress. This was absolutely false.

After hearings had been scheduled, members of the Small Business Subcommittee began to receive telegrams urging that the hearings be postponed thirty days. The sameness of the requests made the lobbying obvious; it indicated a very carefully thought-out plan to kill the subcontracting program proposal outright.

It was against this backdrop that the hearings were held, on March 15–17 and April 24, 1961. It was at these hearings that the first public discussion of the proposed subcontracting program took place.

John Horne, the administrator of SBA, presented the position of the executive branch on the new program. He suggested that the program be "cooperatively developed" by the Defense Department, General Services Administration, and SBA. Most important of all, he suggested that in the event that the agencies could not come to an agreement, the Pentagon and GSA determine the content of their respective regulations on this program. This meant SBA, the small businessman's representative, would be shut out and shut up whenever there was a difference of opinion.

Thus it was clear that the Pentagon, having cabinet status, had worked its will and forced Administration witnesses to agree to a program that would downgrade the role SBA would play in the establishment of the program. Under the Administration proposal, a junior partnership was the best SBA could expect, and they would get that only if the Pentagon and GSA wanted them to have it. The SBA's willingness to agree to an amendment to the bill which would prevent it from taking the lead in the program astounded Senator Sparkman and me, and we voiced our objections to the proposed change very vehemently.

Senator Sparkman remarked, relative to this proposed change:

"What happens to the Small Business Administration? Maybe I read it wrong, but the way I read it, if you are not able to settle, why then SBA just goes out the window.

209

The Small Business Administration drops out and the other two are allowed to carry on."

Later on I said (speaking to the administrator of SBA):

"Let me now go into what I think is a very watered down, mild, meek, and perhaps worthless proposal. Maybe I am too harsh.

"These are the concessions. Instead of having SBA originate the program, a committee originates it.

"SBA gives up its initiative. That is my first objection. SBA had the initiative in the past and the sole initiative.

"In the second place, as Senator Sparkman has brought out so well, SBA would not be in it. It might be in on the conception but would not be in on the birth and bringing up of this child.

"Defense and GSA make the final decision.

"In the third place, I do not see anything here in the bill to provide assurance that the prime contractors will confer with SBA when they are requested to do so.

"This is in the bill that we have, but you stipulated to a compromise which does not include that at all.

"In the fourth place, there is no provision for enabling SBA to obtain from government procurement agencies the data concerning subcontracting. There is no way you can initiate the program or oversee it. You cannot make a final decision on it, and you cannot procure the data which the present bill provides that you can."

Thomas D. Morris, assistant secretary of defense (installations and logistics), expressed his approval of the Administration's proposal. He restated the Pentagon's old objection to the language of the bill, saying that the authority of the Department of Defense over its prime contractors would be diluted, and that it would give SBA too much power over procurement if the language of my amendment were to be adopted.

In the face of this adamant opposition on the part of the Pentagon, as well as the enforced "going along" of SBA, Congress finally passed the Administration amendment. We were able, however, to place in the law the provision that SBA would have to concur in the regulations for the program before they could be published.

I have not given up the fight for an adequate proposal. The watered-down program enacted in 1961 is not sufficient to do the job that must be done.

Sometime during this session of Congress (the 88th), I plan to hold informal hearings of the Small Business Subcommittee to review the present status of this program. Senator Sparkman and I are determined to press for our more hardhitting, effective program. To accomplish this, we may have to knock a few heads together. After my experiences and frustrations with guiding the present subcontracting program through Congress, I might enjoy it!

21

WHERE DO WE GO FROM HERE?

Despite the predictions of its imminent decease, small business in the United States—at least at this writing—refuses to die out. Indeed, like Mark Twain, the reports of its death are exaggerated.

As I pointed out earlier, the over-all number of small businesses in this country, far from diminishing, continues to grow steadily year by year. This is a good sign. It means that the American economy still preserves the climate in which a man or woman can make a start in a new business. Whether or not the climate is as salubrious for small business *survival* is, of course, quite another matter.

The fact is that the same statistics which show an upward curve each year in the number of new small businesses do not reveal that the number of small business failures each year nearly equals the number of small businesses created. This is not a healthy situation. Something is wrong somewhere.

One can be cold-blooded about these statistics. An assistant secretary of commerce once blithely pointed out that while "small companies do go broke—the number of firms going out of business is more than matched by the number of new firms starting up."

This seems to me rather a peculiar attitude: "Let's not worry about the human misery and waste involved in all these business failures, so long as the good old statistics keep climbing upward."

The statistics do, however, have one positive implication. They prove that the average American, in this age of the organization man, has more spirit, daring, and enterprise than we usually give him credit for.

It is to preserve the climate in which this spirit, daring, and enterprise may flourish and, more important, in which it may be *fulfilled,* that the friends of small business in Congress must fight.

It's tough enough to start out in business, but it's even tougher to stay in business—to succeed over the long pull. The creation of a healthy economic climate, in which small business can do both, is essential not only to small business survival, but to the survival of our very way of life.

As is evident from our analysis of small business, the problems of staying in business today have become overwhelming. Most small business entrepreneurs simply do not have much "survival potential."

Among those who do manage to stay in business, many struggle along in a hopeless "twilight zone." They are not slipping backward, perhaps, but they are not making much progress either. While officially recorded as "successful," these businesses might better be termed "non-failures." Because they lack one or more of the essentials for growth—often through no fault of their proprietors—they are doomed to stagnation.

This twilight zone existence frustrates thousands of our fellow citizens who own small businesses or depend upon them for employment. Moreover, it denies to society the skills and talents of literally millions of owners and workers, and impedes the general economic growth.

As I have indicated, it is my strong conviction—bolstered by meeting and talking with thousands of small businessmen in Wisconsin and throughout the nation—that the last thing most small businessmen want is coddling, especially by the federal government.

Indeed, the type of person who wants a secure life with little risk is not the man who goes into business for himself in the first place. Rather, he seeks out a safe corner in some big corporation, rises on the well-marked promotional ladder to his own level, and retires at the prescribed age without ever having risked anything.

Nevertheless, while the vast majority of small businessmen do not ask for special treatment, they do demand—and rightly so—an even break. The deck is stacked in favor of big business, financially, managerially, technically, and governmentally, and each day the situation gets worse. That is why it is so important that

Congress act now. Time is running out for small business in America, and this decade of the sixties will be decisive for its future.

What are the friends of small business in Congress trying to do? Certainly we are not attempting to weight the scales so in favor of small business that it becomes impossible for anyone to fail. Those who serve on the committees dealing with small business problems are, in the main, tough realists who are not inclined to advocate legislation for the small business community out of any false sentimentality. Nor are we the "enemies" of big business. Recognizing the positive contributions each type of business makes to American society, we simply are trying to set small business and big business in balance.

In the beginning chapter, I indicated that in order to give small business an even break three courses of action were necessary. In the first five parts of this book I have tried to indicate two of these courses: to give positive recognition to the contributions which small business makes to the U. S. economy, and to rally the small businessman with all the advice and assistance possible in his perfectly legitimate efforts to grow and prosper.

Neither of these two courses of action will do the job, however, if we fail in a third course, in the crucial sector of public policy. This is the sector which determines the over-all business climate that I have been talking about. In this last section of the book, I have explored in some detail two of the big issues of public policy and small business: taxes and government procurement.

What are some of the other areas where the friends of small business in Congress must go to bat for you? In the main, these areas have all been sketched in the preceding chapters. To sum up briefly, I believe that Congress must do something to enable the small businessman to get the long-term money he needs with the same ease—and at the same low rates of interest—as big business.

Government loan procedures in the Small Business Administration and the affiliated Small Business Investment Companies need to be simplified and streamlined. Personally, I would rather see more money made available by returning again to an $150,000 or $200,000 loan ceiling than by appropriating more and more funds in each session of Congress.

Congress must also urge and assist banks and other private lending agencies to shoulder more of the burden of small business investment. I have suggested a few of the ways in which this could be done in the chapters on banks and SBICs. Ultimately, the private sector of the economy must do the job for small business, even though the Small Business Administration and other government agencies can (and do) render valuable assistance while the equity gap is being closed.

Perhaps even more urgent than the capital crisis is the question of competent management in small busi-

217

ness. As I have pointed out, many observers believe this to be the crux of the small business problem. The capital difficulty, these experts say, is only a manifestation of the deeper lack of management ability. A good manager would solve his financial problems. A bad manager has financial problems precisely because he *is* inefficient.

In the field of management counsel and assistance, Congress, through the executive agencies it has created, is, on the whole, doing a fairly good job for you. This is not to imply that there cannot be a great many improvements. But the large range of management-improvement programs offered by such agencies as the Department of Commerce and the Small Business Administration are, frankly, underused by the small business community. As you and other small businessmen begin to take greater advantage of the management counsel available to you, there will be more impetus and incentive to add to and improve these services. The same thing holds true for the many excellent private management-assistance agencies.

There is little I can add on the question of big business and the antitrust laws. As I mentioned earlier, this is possibly the most crucial economic issue facing Congress in this decade. I wish I could promise great victories for small businessmen in equalizing by law his right to compete. But the interests defending monopoly are powerful, and I am not hopeful that we can very easily turn the tide. What I *can* promise is that those of us in Washington who are engaged in this battle will not give up.

Finally, Congress is determined that American business shall have the opportunity and the incentive to sell abroad. In the field of export, the laws we have made, particularly the revolutionary Trade Expansion Act, and the agencies we have created have the potential to do an excellent job for you. If the American businessman responds to the challenge of new overseas markets, we shall be able to bolster our own economy, solve our balance of payments problem, and score victories on many fronts in the Cold War.

In conclusion, you as a small businessman have a tough road ahead. I hope that some of the suggestions in this book will help you to help yourself. But only you can realize the potential inherent in your own business—that often perplexing, sometimes discouraging, but always challenging business of your own.

INDEX